Insurance Regulation in the United States

Insurance Regulation in the United States

AN OVERVIEW FOR BUSINESS AND GOVERNMENT

Peter M. Lencsis

QUORUM BOOKS
Westport, Connecticut • London

Library of Congress Cataloging-in-Publication Data

Lencsis, Peter M. 1953–
    Insurance regulation in the United States : an overview for
business and government / Peter M. Lencsis.
        p. cm.
    Includes bibliographical references and index.
    ISBN 1–56720–085–0 (alk. paper)
    1. Insurance law—United States. I. Title.
KF1164.3.L46 1997
346.73'086—dc20
[347.30686]   96–32507

British Library Cataloguing in Publication Data is available.

Library of Congress Catalog Card Number: 96–32507
ISBN: 1–56720–085–0

First published in 1997

Quorum Books, 88 Post Road West, Westport, CT 06881
An imprint of Greenwood Publishing Group, Inc.

Printed in the United States of America

The paper used in this book complies with the
Permanent Paper Standard issued by the National
Information Standards Organization (Z39.48–1984).

10 9 8 7 6 5 4 3 2 1

Contents

vi   Contents

Introduction

The insurance business in the United States currently comprises approximately 1,700 life and health insurance companies and 3,300 property-casualty insurance companies. Although many of these companies are commonly owned and managed in ''groups,'' the number of separate insurance underwriting enterprises is still very large in comparison to most other countries. As of 1995, these insurers' combined assets were $2.9 trillion, and their total premiums of $820 billion were the equivalent of almost 11 percent of the gross domestic product of $7.2 trillion. In addition to the insurers themselves, there are a multitude of related businesses and professions, including agency and brokerage operations; actuarial, legal, and accounting functions; and claims adjusting, consulting, administration, and the like. Total employment in the United States insurance industry is estimated at 2.2 million individuals.

In 1995, Japan represented the largest segment, approximately 31 percent, of the world insurance market, measured by premiums. The United States was second with 30 percent, and Germany was third, with 7 percent. In terms of premium as a pecentage of gross domestic product, Japan, South Africa, and South Korea ranked first, second, and third, respectively, in 1995.

Insurance regulation in the United States is extensive and complex, especially because most regulation exists at the individual state level rather than at the federal level. Although there is a substantial amount of standardization, insurers operating in numerous states are still subject to separate and mostly non-uniform requirements pertaining to licensing, investments, rates and forms, taxation, and other matters from one state to another. This non-uniform or ''patchwork'' regulatory scheme, particularly when viewed from a global perspective, has recently led to proposals for a single federal regulatory system, at least with regard to insurer solvency standards and the handling of insurer insolvencies. Nevertheless, the existing state regulatory schemes have a fundamental consistency in their primary objectives, which are insurer solvency, reliability and availability of coverages, and fairness and equity to insurance consumers.

Because the essence of the insurance contract is a promise to provide benefits in the future, perhaps years after the premiums are paid, the essence of insurance regulation is the enforcement of that promise in real, practical terms by making certain that insurers have adequate, liquid funds to pay claims, whether days or decades after the corresponding premiums have been paid. In addition to solvency, insurance regulation is largely devoted to making certain that all legitimate needs for insurance are met, and to promoting fairness and equity on the part of insurers in their dealings with policyholders and claimants, with regard to the content of policies, premium classifications and rates, and marketing and claim practices.

This book is intended for educational and reference use as an introduction to, and overview of, the subject of insurance regulation as it currently exists in the United States. The text begins with the history of state-versus-federal regulation and the enactment of the federal McCarran-Ferguson Act as the centerpiece of insurance regulation in the United States. Next are chapters devoted to the "life cycle" of an insurer, including the formation, organization, and licensing of insurers; regulation of insurer assets and investments; ongoing requirements pertaining to reports and examinations; corporate combinations and changes; and insolvency and liquidation laws. Other chapters discuss requirements relative to policy forms and rates; participation in assigned risk plans and other residual markets; the regulation of agents and brokers; and the special risk management techniques involving self-insurance, non-admitted insurers, and captive insurers. The final chapters discuss regulation of reinsurance and insurers' trade practices, and taxation of insurers.

Although a truly comprehensive study of the subject would require many volumes, it is hoped that this text will fulfill the need on the part of those who regulate, as well as those who are regulated, for a concise and convenient guidebook to this intriguing, albeit sometimes frustrating, regulatory maze.

This book is dedicated to the author's father, Michael J. Lencsis, who was employed by the New Jersey Department of Insurance and its predecessor, the Department of Banking and Insurance, for over 30 years until his death in 1972. The author is grateful to Martin Solomon, Gerard T. Keilman, and Richard P. Keating for reviewing a preliminary version of the manuscript, and to Lillian B. Lencsis for much-needed assistance in word processing.

Insurance Regulation
in the United States

1

Historical Background

CONSTITUTIONAL BACKGROUND; STATE REGULATION BEFORE 1944

Business or trade regulation generally means the imposition of specific governmental controls and standards upon business activities which would otherwise be governed only by the decisions of the business owners, the forces of the marketplace, and general law. In the United States, the federal system of government allows for the possibility of business regulation by the federal government, the individual states, or both. Any conflict or tension between federal and state regimes is generally resolved by the superior power or "supremacy" of the federal government.

The United States Constitution contains several provisions that are fundamental to the subject of business regulation in general, and of insurance regulation in particular. Most important is the Commerce Clause,[1] which gives Congress the power to "regulate commerce with foreign nations, and among the several states." Second is the Supremacy Clause,[2] which provides that the Constitution and federal laws made under it are the "supreme law of the land" and therefore take precedence over conflicting state and local laws. Third is the Tenth Amendment, which provides that the governmental powers not given to the United States by the Constitution are "reserved to," i.e., belong to, the individual states or the people.

Taken together, these provisions have been interpreted over the years by the Supreme Court to mean that: (1) the federal government has the power to regulate interstate commerce; (2) the states have the power to regulate intrastate commerce; and (3) the states have only a "residue of power" to regulate matters which "affect" interstate commerce, and in exercising this residual power they cannot impose any "unreasonable burden" on interstate commerce.[3] Given these provisions, the basic question about the legality of insurance regulation at either the state or federal level must be: is insurance "commerce," as that term is used in the Commerce Clause?

In 1869, the United States Supreme Court held in the case of *Paul v. Virginia*[4] that insurance was not commerce and that the Commerce Clause therefore did not prevent the Commonwealth of Virginia from regulating and taxing New York domestic insurance companies that were doing business in Virginia. The Court reasoned that the making of insurance contracts across state boundaries was not commerce because it did not involve the physical passage of people or commodities. In the words of Justice Field:

Issuing a policy of insurance is not a transaction in commerce. The policies are simple contracts of indemnity against loss by fire, entered into between the corporations and the assured, for a consideration paid by the latter. . . . They are not subjects of trade and barter offered in the market as something having an existence and value independent of the parties to them. They are not commodities to be shipped or forwarded from one State to another, and then put up for sale. They are like other personal contracts between parties which are completed by their signature and the transfer of the consideration.[5]

The Court also observed that the fire insurance policies in question were local rather than interstate transactions because by their terms they became effective only upon delivery in Virginia. As long as the Court's decision in *Paul v. Virginia* remained the law, therefore, the states could enact and enforce laws that regulated interstate as well as intrastate aspects of the insurance business, because the restraints of the Commerce Clause did not apply to that business at all. For more than 70 years after the *Paul* decision, the state legislatures continued to develop insurance regulatory schemes and to put into place most of the basic licensing, examination, and solvency-testing requirements that still exist today.

THE *SOUTH-EASTERN UNDERWRITERS* CASE (1944) AND THE McCARRAN-FERGUSON ACT (1945)

In 1944, *Paul v. Virginia*'s interpretation of "commerce" was rejected completely by the Supreme Court in the case of *United States v. South-Eastern Underwriters Association*.[6] Considering the validity of a criminal antitrust indictment against a large group of fire insurance companies, the Court held that insurance was commerce after all and therefore could be regulated by Congress under the Commerce Clause. In particular, the Court held that the Sherman Act,[7] the basic federal antitrust law that had been enacted in 1890, could be applied to these companies, which had joined together as an association for purposes that included the fixing of premium and commission rates. (Price fixing among competitors is a prime example of an agreement "in restraint of trade" that is prohibited by the Sherman Act.) As a result of the decision, because insurance was considered "commerce," not only did the federal antitrust laws apply for the first time to insurance, but Congress had the power to regulate insurance generally. Therefore, at least theoretically, the states had virtually no such power, because most state regulation would constitute an impermissible "burden" on interstate commerce. In sum, most state insurance regulation was invalidated overnight.

The Court's decision was based upon a more contemporary view of the insurance business, described as follows (in the text of Justice Black's opinion):

Premiums collected from policyholders in every part of the United States flow into these companies for investment. As policies become payable, checks and drafts flow back to the many states where the policyholders reside. The result is a continuous and indivisible stream of intercourse among the states composed of collections of premiums, payments of policy obligations, and the countless documents and communications which are essential to the negotiation and execution of policy contracts.[8]

To support its radically changed view, the Court noted that the size of the insurance business had increased vastly since 1869. It also drew a technical distinction between *South-Eastern Underwriters* and *Paul v. Virginia*, observing that the earlier case concerned the validity of a state statute at a time when Congress had not acted to control the insurance business, whereas the later case involved the validity of a federal law which was, in the Court's view, clearly intended to apply to insurance as well as other businesses.[9]

The *South-Eastern Underwriters* case created a legal and business crisis, and, perhaps predictably, it was quickly followed by Congress's enactment in 1945 of the McCarran-Ferguson Act,[10] which was intended to and did effectively counteract, with some exceptions, the Supreme Court's ruling of the previous year. The Act's provisions can be summarized as follows.

1. Congress declares that it is public policy for state regulation of the business of insurance to continue. In other words, Congress generally does not wish to regulate insurance, but leaves that function to the states.

2. Various laws enacted by Congress could conceivably apply to the business of insurance as well as other businesses. (This is an implied recognition of the Supreme Court's holding that insurance is "commerce" which the federal government has the power to regulate.) The courts should not, however, construe any Act of Congress to apply to the business of insurance unless the act specifically relates to insurance.

3. The Sherman Act, the Clayton Act,[11] and the Federal Trade Commission Act[12] are applicable to the business of insurance, but only "to the extent that such business is not regulated by State law." Notwithstanding this, the Sherman Act remains fully applicable to "any agreement to boycott, coerce, or intimidate, or act of boycott, coercion, or intimidation."

The Sherman Act provides in broad terms that any "contract, combination . . . or conspiracy, in restraint of trade"[13] is illegal, and by judicial interpretation this has come to mean that all "unreasonable" restraints of trade (i.e., unreasonably anti-competitive business combinations) are prohibited.[14] It also provides that any person who monopolizes, attempts to monopolize, or conspires with others to monopolize in trade or commerce is guilty of a crime.[15] (A monopoly can be defined generally as the power to influence prices or exclude competition.[16]) The Clayton Act of 1914 prohibits, among other things, business mergers and other combinations that tend "substantially to lessen competition, or . . . to create a monopoly."[17] It also creates a private cause of action for treble damages against violators of the antitrust laws, in favor of any person harmed by the activities that constitute such violations.[18] The Federal Trade Commission Act, also enacted in 1914, generally prohibits "unfair methods of competition in commerce, and unfair or deceptive acts or practices in commerce," and establishes an independent agency, the Federal Trade Commission, for the purpose of enforcing the provisions of the Act.[19]

INTERPRETATION OF THE McCARRAN-FERGUSON ACT GENERALLY

The McCarran-Ferguson Act has two principal aspects, which may be thought of as two sides of a coin. First, it validates or legitimizes the many activities of state regulation which would otherwise constitute an illegal interference with the sweeping powers of the federal government under the Commerce Clause. Second, it provides a limited federal antitrust immunity to the "business of insurance."

There are in turn two keys to understanding the second, antitrust aspect of the McCarran-Ferguson Act: (1) the phrase "the business of insurance" and (2) the phrase "to the extent not regulated by State law." In order for the antitrust exemption to apply to a particular activity or practice, that activity or practice must be both part of the business of insurance and regulated by state law. The prime example of such a practice is ratemaking by insurers in combination, usually under the umbrella of a "rating organization" (not entirely unlike the South-Eastern Underwriters Association) established and financed by member insurers.

State insurance laws commonly provide that rates for various lines of insurance must conform to certain standards, that they must be filed with the insurance commissioner for approval before they are used, and that such filings may be made by insurers individually or by rating organizations on their behalf. (This subject is discussed in detail in Chapter 7.) As a result, the collective activity of making and agreeing upon prices, or rates, by insurers in this regulated context does not violate the antitrust laws, even if it would otherwise constitute a combination or conspiracy in restraint of trade.

Even if the antitrust exemption of the McCarran-Ferguson Act applies to a particular activity, that exemption is not unlimited. The Sherman Act continues to apply to acts of boycott, coercion, and intimidation without regard to the scope of state regulation. "Boycott" generally means a coordinated refusal to deal with someone, and in this context it has been interpreted to include agreements not to do business with insurance agents, other insurers, and potential purchasers of insurance.[20] "Coercion" and "intimidation" are generally the opposite of a boycott in that they involve a coordinated compulsion of someone to do business, but there is not much law interpreting these terms in this context.[21]

CASES DEFINING "THE BUSINESS OF INSURANCE"

The McCarran-Ferguson Act applies only to "the business of insurance," as stated above, but that phrase is not defined in the Act at all. Since approximately 1969, increasing doubt has developed over the exact meaning of the phrase. A number of cases decided in the federal courts beginning in that year have, however, consistently resulted in a narrowing interpretation of what constitutes "the business of insurance," as opposed to "the insurance business."

First, in *Securities and Exchange Commission v. National Securities, Inc.,*[22] the SEC sought to enforce the anti-fraud provisions of the federal securities laws in connection with a proposed merger of life insurance companies. The defendants contended that the McCarran-Ferguson Act prevented the application of such federal laws to their merger activities because those activities were part of the business of insurance and had been approved by the Arizona Director of Insurance as being in the interest of the stockholders. The Supreme Court held that McCarran-Ferguson did not apply because a state statute intended to protect the interests of investors does not regulate "the business of insurance."

Next, in *Group Life & Health Ins. Co. v. Royal Drug Company,*[23] the Court held in a federal antitrust context that agreements between a health insurer and "participating" pharmacies, where insureds could obtain drugs at reduced rates, were not part of the business of insurance because such agreements did not involve the underwriting or spreading of risk, were not an integral part of the insurer-policyholder relationship, and were not unique to the insurance industry. Similarly, in *Union Labor Life Ins. Co. v. Pireno,*[24] another antitrust case, the Court found that an insurer's use of a peer review committee to evaluate charges for chiropractic services was not the business of insurance, based upon the criteria set forth in the *Royal Drug* case.

Most recently, in *Department of the Treasury v. Fabe,*[25] the Court determined (but only by a bare majority) that the liquidation priority provisions of a state insurance law were not pre-empted by the federal "super-priority" statute, because the state law in question did regulate the "business of insurance." In so doing, the majority of the Court rejected the argument that state insurer liquidation laws regulate only debtor-creditor relationships, not the "business of insurance." Nevertheless, the four justices in the minority believed that the liquidation of an insurer did not involve the spreading of risk and was therefore not part of the "business of insurance." At present, therefore, it appears that the scope of the "business of insurance" is limited to activities that have to do more or less directly with the insurance contract itself, the spreading of economic risk, and other functions that are unique to the business of an insurance company, as opposed to corporate finances, stock purchases, and incidental activities that are common to other industries.

STATE ANTITRUST LAWS AND "MINI-McCARRAN" ACTS

Although the McCarran-Ferguson Act and the federal antitrust laws are of central importance in insurance regulation, state antitrust laws and certain federal judicial doctrines are also significant. Most states have antitrust laws that prohibit such things as "contracts, combinations, and conspiracies in restraint of trade," monopolization and attempts to monopolize, and other anti-competitive practices of the kinds covered by the federal antitrust laws. State antitrust laws usually contain a provision that exempts insurance activities at least partially from their coverage, either by a specific reference to insurance[26] or by a general reference to state-regulated business activities. These exemption provisions are sometimes referred to as "Mini-McCarran Acts," particularly when they refer specifically to insurance.

"STATE ACTION" AND "NOERR-PENNINGTON" DOCTRINES

Even before passage of the McCarran-Ferguson Act, the judicially created "state action" doctrine made the federal antitrust laws inapplicable to certain business activities undertaken to comply with mandatory provisions of state law. This doctrine, which is associated primarily with the Supreme Court's 1943 decision in *Parker v. Brown*,[27] holds that the Sherman Act in particular was not intended to, and therefore does not, apply to business activities that are conducted under a state legislative mandate. (The *Parker* decision itself concerned a California agricultural proration program which artificially controlled the production and sale of most of the California raisin crop. Because the terms of the program were dictated by the state itself, the Court held that there was no contract or agreement that could violate the Sherman Act, but only "state action" consisting of legislation and enforcement.) Although substantial uncertainty exists, it is generally thought that the state action doctrine would, even in the absence of the McCarran-Ferguson Act, immunize certain insurance industry collective activities, such as statistical gathering and ratemaking, if those activities were affirmatively required by state law.[28]

Related to the "state action" doctrine is the "Noerr-Pennington" doctrine, which is derived from two Supreme Court cases, *Eastern Railroad Presidents Conference v. Noerr Motor Freight, Inc.*,[29] and *United Mine Workers v. Pen-*

nington,[30] decided in 1961 and 1965, respectively. This doctrine states generally that collective activities aimed at seeking legislative or regulatory changes are exempt from the application of the antitrust laws, primarily because of the First Amendment's guarantee of freedom of speech. The activities of insurance companies in this regard are no exception.

FUTURE OF THE McCARRAN-FERGUSON ACT

In recent years, there have been various proposals, and bills introduced into Congress, regarding a partial repeal of the McCarran-Ferguson Act, the creation of a federal agency to regulate insurance company solvency, or both. Most of the proposals would still allow insurers to share historical loss information, to cooperate in developing policy forms, and to share residual markets (these features are usually referred to as "safe harbors"). The major impetus for the proposals arises from numerous recent insolvencies, including those of such giant insurers as Executive Life and Mutual Benefit Life, and the perception that state regulation was inadequate to prevent such disasters.[31] As of early 1997, however, Congressional activity in this area is at a virtual standstill, and it appears that there will be no significant federal regulatory developments in the immediate future.

NOTES

1. U.S. Constitution, Art. I, Sec. 8.
2. U.S. Constitution, Art. IV.
3. See, e.g., *Southern Pacific Co. v. Alabama*, 325 U.S. 761 (1945); *Pike v. Bruce Church, Inc.*, 397 U.S. 137 (1970).
4. 8 Wall. 168 (1868).
5. *Id.* at 183.
6. 322 U.S. 533 (1944).
7. 15 U.S.C. Sec. 1 et seq.
8. 322 U.S. at 541.
9. *Id.* at 544–545.
10. 15 U.S.C. Sec. 1011 et seq. (See Appendix 2 for the full text of the Act.)
11. *Id.* Sec. 12 et seq.
12. *Id.* Sec. 41 et seq.
13. *Id.* Sec. 1.
14. See. e.g., *Standard Oil Co. v. U.S.*, 222 U.S. 1 (1911).
15. 15 U.S.C. Sec. 2.
16. See, e.g., *U.S. v. E.I. DuPont de Nemours & Co.*, 351 U.S. 377 (1956).
17. 15 U.S.C. Sec. 2.
18. *Id.* Sec. 15.
19. *Id.* Secs. 41 and 45.
20. *St. Paul Fire & Marine Ins. Co. v. Barry*, 438 U.S. 531 (1978).

21. See Ill. Ins. Dept., *Insurance Regulation and Antitrust: The Effect of the Repeal of the McCarran-Ferguson Act* (1979), pp. 8–10.

22. 393 U.S. 453 (1969).

23. 440 U.S. 205 (1979).

24. 458 U.S. 119 (1982).

25. 113 S.Ct. 2202 (1993).

26. See, e.g., N.Y. Gen. Bus. Law Sec. 340(2).

27. 317 U.S. 341 (1943).

28. Ill. Ins. Dept., supra note 21, pp. 11–13.

29. 365 U.S. 127 (1961).

30. 381 U.S. 657 (1965).

31. See U.S. House of Representatives, Committee on Energy and Commerce, Subcommittee on Oversight, *Failed Promises: Insurance Company Insolvencies* (February 1990).

2

State versus Federal Insurance Regulation

FEDERAL REGULATION OF BANKING, SECURITIES, AND EMPLOYEE BENEFITS; LIABILITY RISK RETENTION ACT; HEALTH INSURANCE COVERAGES

Although insurance regulation has been left largely or mostly to the states since 1945, as it was before the *South-Eastern Underwriters* decision (see Chapter 1), there are several important areas of mostly indirect or tangential federal regulation. These areas include banking, securities, employee benefits, and liability risk retention. There is also some direct federal regulation of health insurance coverages. In addition, various federal insurance programs have been established, ranging from the vast Social Security System to relatively small, specialized programs that provide flood and crime insurance in certain communities where the private insurance market may not satisfy local needs.

There is a fundamental policy, reflected in federal and state laws, which favors keeping the banking business separate from other areas of commerce, including securities and insurance. In very general terms, the primary federal sources of restrictions on banking entities with regard to insurance sales (that is, acting as an insurance agency) or underwriting activities (that is, actual risk-taking) are: (1) the National Bank Act, which limits the authority of national banks to banking and "such incidental powers as may be necessary to carry on the business of banking";[1] (2) the Bank Holding Company Act,[2] which generally prohibits bank holding companies from owning or controlling any non-banking activity; and (3) the amendments to the Bank Holding Company Act made by the Garn–St. Germain Act of 1982.[3] By virtue of a set of intricate exemptions and exceptions set forth in federal statutes, regulations, and agency interpretations, banking entities can engage in certain specified insurance activities, such as the sale of credit insurance in connection with loans, the sale of property insurance on loan collateral, and the sale of insurance generally in small towns (with populations of 5,000 or less) and by small holding companies (with assets of $50 million or less). State banking laws also restrict the ability of state-chartered banks to become involved in the insurance business.

Examples of state laws which prevent insurers from engaging in the banking business are: Section 1701 of the New York Insurance Law, which generally prohibits a domestic life insurer from organizing or holding a bank, trust company, savings and loan association, or savings bank as a subsidiary; and Section 1601 of the New York law, which effectively limits domestic property-casualty companies to investments in subsidiaries that engage in activities "ancillary to an insurance business."[4]

Since the 1930's, the securities industry in the United States has been highly regulated, especially with regard to assuring full and adequate disclosure of all relevant information to investors. In particular, the Securities Act of 1933[5] requires a "registration statement" to be filed with a federal agency, the Securities and Exchange Commission (SEC), before most "securities" can be sold in interstate commerce; its definition of "security" excludes "any insurance or endowment policy or annuity contract . . . issued by a corporation subject to the supervision of the insurance commissioner . . . of any State."[6]

Some insurance contracts (primarily life and annuity products, such as variable life and annuities, whose payouts are based on the fluctuating value of investment portfolios) are so much like non-insurance investments that they are considered "securities" under the Securities Act, despite the above-quoted exclusion. Also, the companies that sell these products may be considered "issuers" of securities and "investment companies" under the Investment Company Act of 1940,[7] which requires investment companies to be registered with the SEC before they can offer their shares for sale in interstate commerce. The relevant test, as stated in the 1958 case of *Securities and Exchange Commission v. Variable Annuity Life Insurance Co.*,[8] is whether the insurance contracts contain "very substantial" or "predominant" investment aspects so that they are no longer insurance or annuity contracts which qualify for exemptions from the federal acts. Insurance products that are considered securities are subject to a multitude of disclosure and similar requirements in addition to registration under the federal laws and regulations.

The result of the applicability of securities laws to certain insurance contracts is, in effect, a dual system of regulation whereby the securities aspects of those products are regulated by the federal government, and their insurance aspects are regulated by state law. The state laws accommodate the unique aspects of so-called "registered products" by allowing for the creation of "separate accounts" for life insurers (see Chapter 4). These laws permit an insurer's book of variable business to be treated for accounting purposes as virtually a separate "company within a company."

In the field of employee benefits, a complex and far-reaching federal law, the

Employee Retirement Income Security Act of 1974 (ERISA),[9] establishes vesting and funding requirements for private pension plans and generally regulates the design of pension and other benefit plans. It preempts (i.e., supersedes) state laws insofar as they relate to most plans,[10] but due to its "savings clause"[11] it does not preempt state laws which regulate insurance, banking, or securities. Nevertheless, ERISA's "deemer clause"[12] generally prevents the states from deeming (i.e., considering) an employee benefit plan to be an insurance company, bank, or investment company, or an entity engaged in the business of insurance or banking, for the purpose of regulating it. ERISA also established the Pension Benefit Guaranty Corporation,[13] a federal entity which guarantees that certain vested portions of pension benefits will be available to plan participants and beneficiaries in the event of termination of a defined benefit pension plan.

Another body of federal law, the Consolidated Omnibus Budget Reconciliation Act (COBRA),[14] requires many employers to provide continuation of health insurance coverages for terminating employees and certain family members for periods that range from 18 to 36 months after termination of employment. The continued coverages cannot be conditioned upon insurability of the persons involved, and the employer cannot charge more than 102 percent of what comparable coverages cost for active employees. Yet another federal law relating to health insurance plans is the Health Maintenance Organization (HMO) Act of 1973,[15] which required certain employers to offer HMO membership to employees as an alternative to more traditional plans, and which also provided initial financial assistance for the development of HMOs (see Chapter 3 for a discussion of HMOs).

In the property-casualty field, the federal Product Liability Risk Retention Act of 1981[16] was enacted during the "liability crisis" to allow businesses to create risk retention groups and purchasing groups under state supervision for product liability risks. The scope of the Act was expanded in 1986 to include most lines of commercial liability insurance other than workers' compensation,[17] and the legislation is now known as the Liability Risk Retention Act. The organization of such groups was intended as an alternative to the conventional purchase of liability insurance during a period of very high rates and limited insurer capacity.

Some states have enacted supplemental regulatory laws to govern the formation and operation of such risk retention and purchasing groups (see Chapter 12). These laws may provide for the licensing or registration of individual groups, for periodic financial reports to the state regulator, and for the payment of franchise and premium taxes.[18]

Finally, a federal law[19] sets forth minimum standards and requirements (including loss ratios) for Medicare Supplement policies, based largely upon National Association of Insurance Commissioners (NAIC) model standards. This federal law permits insurers to comply under a state regulatory program which has been certified by the Secretary of Health and Human Services. Even though this law recognizes and interrelates with state regulation, it nevertheless represents a rare instance of direct federal involvement in the pricing and content of insurance coverage.

SOCIAL SECURITY AND OTHER FEDERAL INSURANCE PROGRAMS

There are some federal insurance programs of relatively limited scope, and others of huge proportions. The National Flood Insurance Act of 1968[20] and the Flood Disaster Protection Act of 1973[21] provide for the availability of flood and mudslide coverage to certain property owners in all states. The National Flood Insurance Program is administered jointly by private insurers and the Federal Insurance Administration (FIA), and as of 1995 it provided coverage under 3.3 million policies in approximately 18,000 communities which have identified special flood hazard areas.[22]

The Federal Crime Insurance Program, administered by the Federal Insurance Administrator, provided burglary and robbery coverages in about ten states, the District of Columbia, and the Virgin Islands, based upon a determination that such coverages were unavailable locally. Approximately 17,000 policies were written through the program as of 1994.[23] The program was discontinued in 1995. The Federal Crop Insurance Program, also administered by the FIA, provides multiple-peril crop insurance at subsidized rates for crop losses resulting from such things as hail, wind, excessive rain, freezing, and drought.[24] Two other substantial programs, Federal Employees Group Life Insurance (FEGLI) and Servicemen's Group Life Insurance (SGLI), provide life insurance to civilian and military employees of the United States, respectively.[25]

The federal Social Security Act[26] was originally enacted in 1935 during the Great Depression. The programs covered by the Act include: (1) retirement, survivors, and disability insurance (sometimes referred to as OASDI or Old Age, Survivors, and Disability Insurance); (2) hospital and medical insurance for the aged, the disabled, and certain persons with kidney disease (Medicare); (3) unemployment insurance; (4) black lung benefits for certain coal miners and others in related employments; and (5) supplemental security income (SSI).[27] Social Security expenditures are a highly publicized subject, running in the hundreds of billions of dollars annually and comprising a substantial part of the federal budget.

STATE INSURANCE REGULATORS AND THE NATIONAL ASSOCIATION OF INSURANCE COMMISSIONERS (NAIC)

Each state of the United States, as well as the District of Columbia, Puerto Rico, the Virgin Islands, Guam, and American Samoa, has within its executive branch of government an insurance regulatory official. These officials are usually called "commissioners," "superintendents," or "directors" of insurance, and they are listed by state in Table 2.1. The commonly accepted generic term for such officials, regardless of their actual titles, is "commissioner."

Table 2.1
Insurance Regulatory Officials (E = Elected; all others are appointed)

Alabama	Commissioner of Insurance
Alaska	Director of Insurance
American Samoa	Insurance Commissioner, Office of the Governor
Arizona	Director of Insurance
Arkansas	Insurance Commissioner
California	Commissioner of Insurance (E)
Colorado	Commissioner of Insurance
Connecticut	Commissioner of Insurance
Delaware	Insurance Commissioner (E)
District of Columbia	Commissioner of Insurance
Florida	Insurance Commissioner (E)
Georgia	Insurance Commissioner
Guam	Insurance Commissioner
Hawaii	Insurance Commissioner
Idaho	Director of Insurance
Illinois	Commissioner of Insurance
Indiana	Commissioner of Insurance
Iowa	Commissioner of Insurance
Kansas	Commissioner of Insurance (E)
Kentucky	Insurance Commissioner
Louisiana	Commissioner of Insurance (E)
Maine	Superintendent of Insurance
Maryland	Insurance Commissioner
Massachusetts	Commissioner of Insurance
Michigan	Commissioner of Insurance
Minnesota	Commissioner of Commerce
Mississippi	Commissioner of Insurance (E)
Missouri	Director of Insurance
Montana	Commissioner of Insurance (E)
Nebraska	Director of Insurance
Nevada	Commissioner of Insurance
New Hampshire	Insurance Commissioner
New Jersey	Commissioner of Banking and Insurance
New Mexico	Superintendent of Insurance
New York	Superintendent of Insurance
North Carolina	Commissioner of Insurance (E)
North Dakota	Commissioner of Insurance (E)
Ohio	Director of Insurance
Oklahoma	Insurance Commissioner (E)
Oregon	Commissioner of the Department of Consumer and Business Services
Pennsylvania	Insurance Commissioner
Puerto Rico	Commissioner of Insurance
Rhode Island	Insurance Commissioner
South Carolina	Insurance Commissioner
South Dakota	Director of Insurance
Tennessee	Commissioner of Insurance
Texas	Commissioner of Insurance

Table 2.1 Continued

Utah	Commissioner of Insurance
Vermont	Commissioner of Insurance
Virgin Islands	Director of Insurance
Virginia	Commissioner of Insurance
Washington	Insurance Commissioner (E)
West Virginia	Insurance Commissioner
Wisconsin	Commissioner of Insurance
Wyoming	Insurance Commissioner

The office of insurance commissioner, and the department or other subdivision of the state executive branch which he or she heads, is usually created by statute.[28] Most commissioners are appointed by the governor, sometimes with the "advice and consent" of the state legislature or one of its houses, and in such cases they normally serve at the governor's pleasure (i.e., until they are dismissed by the governor). Some commissioners, particularly in the southern states, are publicly elected for a term of office which is usually coextensive with that of the governor.[29] At the present time, eleven states elect their insurance commissioner, while in the remaining states and jurisdictions the governor or another official appoints the commissioner (see Table 2.1).

The powers and responsibilities of an insurance commissioner, like those of various other executive officials, are actually a mixture of executive, legislative, and judicial functions. Primarily, an insurance commissioner is charged with executing (i.e., carrying out and enforcing) the provisions of state law which regulate the insurance business, such as licensing and examination requirements; but he or she also has substantial quasi-legislative rule-making authority and the authority to act in a quasi-judicial capacity in conducting hearings and rendering decisions in disputed matters.

In many states, the commissioner is granted a broad statutory authority to promulgate rules and regulations, and to decide controversies, in order to carry out the provisions of the insurance laws.[30] Ordinarily this authority is circumscribed by the provisions of a state Administrative Procedures Act (APA) which regulates the rule-making and adjudicative processes in various ways.[31] For example, the APA usually requires the publication of proposed rules, public hearings before the rules are adopted, and basic procedural rules for fairness and efficiency in adjudicative matters.

The insurance code or the APA, or both, may also regulate the hearing and decision-making process in more particular ways,[32] many of which are related to constitutional "due process" requirements, such as prior notice of hearings, the opportunity to be heard and present evidence, and the right to cross-examine witnesses. Examples of matters which might be the subject of an insurance department hearing are license revocation proceedings, rate filings, takeovers of domestic insurers, and instances of alleged unfair trade or claims practices.

Insurance department operations are usually funded through a combination of taxes and fees payable directly to some departments, general state revenues, and

Table 2.2
Organization of a Typical Insurance Department

COMMISSIONER

DEPUTY COMMISSIONER   GENERAL COUNSEL

ADMINISTRATION
Budget
Personnel
Information Systems

COMPANIES DIVISION
Financial Analysis
Actuarial Analysis
Tax
Surplus Lines
Liquidation

COMPANY EXAMINATIONS
Financial
Market Conduct

LICENSING
Companies
Agents & Brokers

RATES AND POLICIES
Property & Casualty Actuarial
Life & Health Actuarial

CONSUMER SERVICES
Investigations
Hearings

special assessments against insurers for some departments' expenses. There is no particular uniformity among the states in this area. The size of insurance department staffs varies from hundreds of persons in states like New York or California to perhaps a few dozen at most in a relatively non-populous state or territory. The organizational structure of a typical insurance department is shown in Table 2.2.

The National Association of Insurance Commissioners (NAIC) was organized in 1871 and was known as the National Convention of Insurance Commissioners until 1935, when the present name was adopted. Its membership currently includes the insurance regulatory officials of all states, the District of Columbia, Puerto Rico, the Virgin Islands, Guam, and American Samoa. The principal officers of the NAIC are its President, a Vice President and Chair of its Executive Committee, a Vice Chair of the Executive Committee, and a Recording Secretary. The NAIC currently maintains a permanent Support Services Office in Kansas City, Missouri, and a Securities Valuation Office (see Chapter 4) in New York City.

The basic organizational structure of the NAIC is shown in Table 2.3. The operations of the NAIC are largely carried out by its committees, subcommittees, and task forces at the NAIC's quarterly meetings, which are regularly attended by many regulatory officials and personnel, insurance company executives, attorneys, actuaries, accountants, and others involved in the insurance industry. The committees are broken down into task forces and are charged with studying various issues, and drafting model laws and regulations where necessary.

The NAIC publishes manuals or handbooks containing detailed instructions for the completion of insurers' annual statements and for the examination of insurers by insurance department representatives (see Chapter 6). These manuals or handbooks, although they do not have the force of law, create for all practical purposes a pattern of uniformity throughout the United States. The NAIC has numerous other publications, including transcripts of the proceedings of its meetings and the *Journal of Insurance Regulation*, which provides a forum for discussion and the results of research on insurance regulatory issues.

In addition to its manuals, an extremely important influence exerted by the NAIC is the adoption of its model laws and regulations, of which there are currently over 150. These models are not of any binding effect unless and until they are adopted, with or without changes, by the legislature or commissioner of a given jurisdiction. They have been so adopted to such an extent that they currently provide a critical fabric of quasi-uniformity among the various U.S. jurisdictions. NAIC model laws and regulations represent an immense cooperative effort by representatives of many U.S. jurisdictions, and they are the source of many of the relatively standardized laws and regulations that are discussed in this text.

Largely as a result of congressional criticism of non-uniform and supposedly uncoordinated state regulatory activity, the NAIC has recently developed an "accreditation" program under which it grants or withholds accreditation of individual state insurance departments, based upon a combination of (1) each respective state's conformity with certain "key" model laws and regulations and (2) each department's funding and organizational adequacy. As of early 1997, although 48 states have been accredited, New York is a conspicuously non-accredited department, due primarily to the state legislature's refusal to enact certain measures. The NAIC initially intended to impose certain penalties or disadvantages upon non-accredited departments, but has recently abandoned that approach to the promotion of its goals.

Table 2.3
NAIC Committee Structure

I. PLENARY SESSION

II. EXECUTIVE COMMITTEE

III. COMMITTEES OF THE EXECUTIVE COMMITTEE

Committee on Financial Regulation
Committee on Credit Insurance
Special Committee on Information Systems
Special Committee on Blue Cross Plans
Special Committee on Antifraud
Special Committee on Health Care Reform
Casualty Actuarial (Technical) Task Force
Life & Health Actuarial (Technical) Task Force

IV. STANDING COMMITTEES

Life Insurance Committee
Accident and Health Insurance Committee
      Long-Term Care Insurance Task Force
      Medicare Supplement & Other Limited Benefit Plans Task Force
      Senior Counseling Activities Task Force
      State & Federal Health Insurance Legislative Policy Task Force
Personal Lines P&C Insurance Committee
Commercial Lines P&C Committee
      Statistical Task Force
      Workers' Compensation Task Force
Special Insurance Issues Committee
      International Insurance Relations Task Force
      Reinsurance Task Force
      Surplus Lines Task Force

V. STANDING SUBCOMMITTEES

Internal Administration Subcommittee
      Education, Research & Training Task Force
Zone Coordination Subcommittee
Market Conduct & Consumer Affairs Subcommittee
      Insurance Availability and Affordability Task Force
      Market Conduct Examination Oversight Task Force
Financial Condition Subcommittee
      Accounting Practices & Procedures Task Force
      Blanks Task Force
      Examination Oversight Task Force
      Guaranty Fund Task Force
      Rehabilitators and Liquidators Task Force
      Valuation of Securities Task Force
Insolvency Subcommittee
Financial Regulation Standards and Accreditation Subcommittee

NOTES

1. 12 U.S.C. Sec. 24.
2. *Id.* Sec. 1843.
3. 12 U.S.C. Sec. 1843(c)(8).
4. The regulation of combined banking-insurance activities, by banking and insurance entities, at both the state and federal levels is an intricate and rapidly-changing area of law which cannot be adequately explored in this text. For a fuller discussion see chapter 20, "Insurance and Banking," *New York Insurance Law* (New York: Matthew Bender & Co., 1995). Note: Banking is subject to an extremely complex, dual state-and-federal regulatory system in the United States; this fact further complicates the interplay between banking and insurance regulation.
5. 15 U.S.C. Sec. 77a et seq.
6. *Id.* Sec. 77c(8).
7. *Id.* Sec. 80a-1 et seq.
8. 359 U.S. 65 (1959).
9. P.L. 93–406; 29 U.S.C. Sec. 1001 et seq.
10. 29 U.S.C. Sec. 1144(a).
11. *Id.* Sec. 1144(b)(2)(A).
12. *Id.* Sec. 1144(b)(2)(B).
13. *Id.* Sec. 1301 et seq.
14. P.L. 99–272.
15. P.L. 93–222.
16. P.L. 97–45.
17. P.L. 99–563.
18. See, e.g., N.Y. Ins. Law Sec. 5901 et seq.
19. 42 U.S.C. Sec. 1395ss.
20. P.L. 90–448 Title XIII.
21. P.L. 93–234.
22. *1997 Property-Casualty Fact Book* (New York: Insurance Information Institute, 1997), p. 46.
23. *Id.* p. 48.
24. Rejda, *Principles of Risk Management and Insurance*, 5th ed. (New York: HarperCollins College Publishers, 1995), p. 174.
25. *Id.* pp. 106 and 293.
26. 42 U.S.C. Sec. 401 et seq.
27. *Social Security Manual* (Cincinnati: National Underwriter Co., 1995), p. 1.
28. See, e.g., N.Y. Ins. Law Sec. 201.
29. *Id.*
30. See, e.g., N.Y. Ins. Law Sec. 301.
31. See, e.g., N.Y. State Administrative Procedures Act, Sec. 201 et seq.
32. *Id.* Sec. 301 et seq.

3

Formation and Organization of Insurers

INCORPORATION GENERALLY

Virtually all insurance companies in the United States are incorporated business entities that possess the distinctive "corporate" attribute of limited liability. Originally, under British and American law a corporation or "limited liability company" could be created only by a special act of the parliament or legislature, which granted to the company a legal "personality" separate from that of its shareholder-owners, so that the debts and other obligations of the company were solely its own, and not enforceable against the shareholders. This status was embodied in a "charter" which became the legal document underlying the corporation's existence.

Nowadays legislative charters are rare, and private citizens can create corporations with limited liability, for the purpose of engaging in almost any lawful business enterprise, simply by following the incorporation procedure and filing requirements contained in the general corporation law of a given state.[1] Ordinarily that procedure consists of filing articles of incorporation with the Secretary of State, and paying a nominal incorporation tax or fee, such as $100. There is usually no discretion on the part of the Secretary of State to deny or withhold the corporate status, unless it appears that the corporation is being formed for some purpose other than a "lawful business," or that the corporate name is misleading, or too similar to that of another corporation already in existence.[2] There are generally no requirements as to the amount or kinds of assets or capital the new corporation must have or maintain, and no restrictions on who can be shareholders, directors, or officers.

By contrast, an insurance company cannot ordinarily be formed or organized in any meaningful way under a general corporation law. Instead, insurers are usually formed under the organizational provisions of the state insurance law, or under a combination of provisions from the insurance law and the corporation law. In most states, the general corporation law does apply (with specified exceptions) to the formation and ongoing affairs of an insurance company, but only to the extent that it does not conflict with the insurance law.[3]

STOCK, MUTUAL, AND RECIPROCAL INSURERS

The first step in incorporating an insurance company is to decide whether the form of ownership should be stock or mutual. Stock ownership refers to the usual form of corporate ownership under which the shareholders, who are investing money in the corporation, buy share certificates that entitle them to various kinds of voting rights with regard to the corporation's affairs, certain rights to dividends out of the corporation's profits, and the rights to remaining assets in the event of liquidation. Thus the form of ownership of an insurance company being organized by entrepreneurs as a profit-making venture will normally be the stock form.

A mutual insurance company, on the other hand, has no shareholders or stockholders because it has no shares of stock to issue; instead, the capital and surplus of the company are considered to be owned and controlled by its policyholders as that group of persons may be constituted at certain points in time, or over certain periods of time. For example, the policyholders entitled to vote for directors at a given annual meeting may be those whose policies are in force and have been in force for at least one year.[4] For purposes of liquidation, those who have been policyholders for a certain number of years prior to the liquidation may be entitled to any remaining assets, in proportion to the premiums paid by them.[5]

Thus, in theory at least, a mutual insurance company is a cooperative enterprise, not operated for profit as such, but for the mutual advantage of its various members. Any gains from operations are used to bolster the company's surplus, or returned to the policyholders as policy dividends. In recent years, mutual companies have typically been formed by groups of physicians or other practitioners to provide themselves with liability insurance which would otherwise be difficult or impossible to obtain. The mutual form of organization may also be used by industrial companies or other business entities in creating "captive" insurers as discussed in Chapter 12.

Reciprocal insurers are roughly similar in concept to mutuals. A reciprocal may be defined as an aggregation of persons, corporations, or public entities called "subscribers" who engage, under a common name, in inter-insurance (that is, they insure each other) through an "attorney-in-fact" who has authority to bind the entire body of subscribers to insurance contracts with individual subscribers as policyholders.[6]

Some United States jurisdictions allow the formation of insurance syndicates, composed of individuals and patterned to one extent or another on the operations of Lloyds in Great Britain. These insurers are commonly known as "Lloyds" or "American Lloyds." They should not be confused with the British Lloyds organization, which may have a licensing status or a "white list" status as a surplus lines insurer (see Chapter 10) in certain states.

LIFE-HEALTH AND PROPERTY-CASUALTY INSURERS

Another initial step in the incorporation of an insurance company is determining whether the company will be a life insurance company or a property-casualty company. As a rule in the United States, it must be either one or the other. There is, however, an area of partial overlap which is usually referred to as "accident and health" (or in some states, "disability") insurance which may be transacted by either a life or a property-casualty company, or in some states by a distinct species of company called an accident and health company.[7]

It should be obvious that a life insurance company is one authorized to write life insurance, and that a property-casualty company is one authorized to write property or casualty insurance or both, but this is just the beginning of the distinction. Exactly what lines or subcategories of insurance within the two broad categories can legally be written by different kinds of companies, or by companies with different financial structures, is usually determined with reference to an insurer's licensing status for one or more of the various statutory categories or "lines" of insurance.

The New York Insurance Law's definitions of various lines of insurance are very detailed, as discussed in Chapter 4, and they are primarily applicable to statutory licensing requirements, as distinguished from organizational requirements. The important point for organizational purposes is that, in New York, for example, only a life insurance company can be licensed to write the lines called "life insurance" and "annuities," whereas only a property-casualty company can be licensed to write most of the other lines.

Authorization to write particular lines of insurance is frequently conditioned upon meeting certain specified minimum surplus requirements. For example, a stock property-casualty insurer organized under New York law (a New York "domestic" company) must have at least $500,000 in capital and $250,000 in surplus to write workers' compensation insurance, but it must have at least $900,000 in capital and $450,000 in surplus to write fidelity and surety insurance.[8] (As a practical matter, most insurers meet these requirements many times over.)

The NAIC has recently developed certain "Risk-Based Capital" formulas which establish minimum amounts of capital needed by insurers based upon their respective size and risk characteristics, including asset risk (default and/or fluctuation in value), credit risk associated with receivables (including reinsurance), underwriting risk, and interest-rate risk.

INCORPORATION AND LICENSING UNDER STATE INSURANCE LAW

The incorporators of an insurance company generally must be a specified number of individuals, such as twelve or thirteen.[9] These incorporators must file an application with the applicable state's insurance commissioner stating, among other things, the proposed name of the company, its proposed charter, the kinds of insurance it will write, its principal office location, the number and manner of electing its directors, and the amount of its capital.[10] Usually a notice of intent to incorporate must be published for a number of weeks in a newspaper of general circulation.[11] If the application conforms to the requirements of the statute, under some laws the commissioner must, and under other laws may, issue a certificate of incorporation,[12] but such issuance does not necessarily constitute a license to do business in the state. Such variations from one state to another will obviously influence the incorporators in their choice of a state of domicile for the company.

The discretion, if any, vested in the regulator is usually governed by fairly broad criteria which relate to the "best interests of the people of the state," or some similar statutory formula.[13] The discretion usually applies at least at the licensing stage. Incorporation ordinarily must be followed by licensing (also called "admission," "authorization," or "qualification") to do business in one or more states. The subjects of what constitutes "doing an insurance business" generally, what constitutes doing such a business within a particular state, and the licensing requirements themselves, are discussed in Chapter 4.

ELECTION OF DIRECTORS: STOCK VERSUS MUTUAL INSURERS

The ultimate responsibility for management of an insurance company, like that of any other corporation, belongs to the board of directors, which can be thought of as the corporation's "brain." Directors are the elected representatives of the owners of the corporation, whether stockholders or policyholders. The directors make major decisions and periodically elect officers to run the day-to-day business of the company.

A unique aspect of mutual insurance companies under some laws is the method of electing directors by the policyholders. Whereas stock insurance companies' directors are normally elected by the stockholders on the basis of a vote in proportion to the number of shares owned, some kind of different voting formula is necessary for policyholder voting in a mutual company since there are no shares. In New York, for example, mutual company policyholders' votes are given the following weights: (1) for domestic property-casualty companies, as specified in the charter or bylaws (subject to regulatory approval), on the basis of the amount of insurance held, or any other "fair and equitable" basis, provided that every policyholder must have at least one vote and no policyholder may have more than ten votes;[14] and (2) for domestic life companies, on the basis of one vote per policyholder (including group policyholders), regardless of the number of policies or contracts held, or the amount of insurance purchased. The New York statute also contains extremely detailed provisions regarding the nomination of directors and the solicitation and voting of proxies, the fairly obvious purpose of which is to promote greater opportunity for policyholder participation in elections.[15]

HEALTH MAINTENANCE ORGANIZATIONS (HMOs) AND NON-PROFIT HEALTH INSURERS

In addition to stock and mutual companies, there are a number of other, more specialized, kinds of insurers. A health maintenance organization (HMO) may be broadly defined as an entity that (1) directly or indirectly provides health care services to enrolled members in exchange for a fixed prepayment, and (2) is responsible for the availability and quality of the services provided. HMOs are regulated under special provisions of the insurance laws or other statutes in some states, and the scope of these laws often comprises licensing, examinations, and annual reports.[16] For example, in New York, HMOs are licensed and generally regulated by the Commissioner of Health under Article 44 of the Public Health Law, but their contracts with "enrollees" are subject to regulation by the Superintendent of Insurance.[17]

Non-profit health insurers, primarily members of the Blue Cross and Blue Shield system, are also subject to special regulatory provisions in many states. In New York, for example, they must be organized under the state's Not-for-Profit Corporation Law and licensed by the Department of Insurance, and they must receive the Department's approval of their contract forms and rates.[18]

INSURANCE EXCHANGES

Laws concerning the organization and operation of insurance exchanges exist in New York,[19] Illinois,[20] and Florida.[21] Insurance exchanges in the United States were modeled to a large extent on Lloyds of London, and in that respect they were primarily concerned with property-casualty insurance and their members or "syndicates" could transact either direct insurance or reinsurance. The New York Insurance Exchange was able to write all kinds of reinsurance, direct insurance on non-U.S. risks, and direct insurance on domestic risks that could not be placed in the "Free Trade Zone" (see Chapter 7).

Although the insurance exchanges were devised during a period of undercapacity in the property-casualty market, by the time they began to function the market had turned into one of overcapacity, and the quality of the business written on the exchanges therefore declined substantially. Many underwriting syndicates on the New York exchange became insolvent, and that exchange ceased doing new business in 1987. Likewise, the Insurance Exchange of the Americas (Miami) ceased operations in the late 1980's.

SAVINGS BANK LIFE INSURANCE (SBLI)

The laws of New York, Connecticut, and Massachusetts permit mutual savings banks to establish and maintain life insurance "departments," and through them to sell relatively limited amounts of life insurance (such as $50,000 on any one life) to their customers. Two distinctive features of this so-called savings bank life insurance (or SBLI) are (1) the direct marketing methods used, without the involvement of any agents or brokers, and (2) the "pooling" of mortality risks by all SBLI departments within a state, in order to avoid the impact of adverse fluctuations on any one bank's department.[22] The combined assets of all three SBLI departments were $2.6 billion as of 1995.[23]

NOTES

1. See, e.g., N.Y. Bus. Corp. Law Sec. 401 et seq.
2. *Id.* Sec. 301.
3. *Id.* Sec. 103 and see N.Y. Ins. Law Sec. 108.
4. See N.Y. Ins. Law Sec. 4210 (applicable to domestic mutual life companies).
5. See N.Y. Ins. Law Sec. 7434(d) (surplus distributed to policyholders who were such for five years previous to cessation of issuance of policies).
6. See N.Y. Ins. Law Sec. 107(a)(37) and Sec. 6101 et seq.
7. *Id.* Sec. 107(a)(1).
8. N.Y. Ins. Law Sec. 4103(a).
9. *Id.* Sec. 1201(a).
10. *Id.*
11. *Id.* Subsection (a)(3).
12. *Id.* Subsection (a)(6).
13. N.Y. Ins. Law Sec. 1102(d).
14. *Id.* Sec. 4116.
15. *Id.* Sec. 4210(b)(3).
16. *Id.* Sec. 4210(c)-(m).
17. N.J.S.A. 17B:18–18 et seq.
18. N.Y. Public Health Law Sec. 4406.
19. See N.Y. Ins. Law Sec. 4301 et seq.
20. N.Y. Ins. Law Sec. 6201 et seq.
21. Ill. Ins. Code Sec. 107.01 et seq.
22. Fla. Ins. Code Sec. 629.401.
23. *1996 Life Insurance Fact Book* (Washington, D.C.: American Council of Life Insurance, 1996), p. 122.

4

Licensing of Insurers

LICENSING GENERALLY

As discussed in Chapter 1, each state of the United States has the power under the Constitution to regulate "intrastate" commerce, that is, business activities which take place within its own borders. The states are also authorized by Congress under the McCarran-Ferguson Act to regulate the "business of insurance" in its interstate aspects, that is, with regard to matters that constitute or affect interstate commerce and that would be, in the absence of the Act, beyond their powers of regulation.

State regulation of this interstate insurance business must, however, be limited to aspects of that business in which the respective states have a substantial and legitimate territorial interest.[1] In other words, any particular state must have a sufficient interest, usually based on some "contacts" or "situs" within its geographical limits, with respect to the business being regulated in order for the regulation to be valid. (This is also generally true with regard to regulation of other kinds of businesses.)

The three most important issues involved in licensing of insurers on a state-by-state basis are: (1) whether the insurer in question is "doing business" or "engaged in business" in a particular state; (2) whether the business being engaged in is the insurance business, namely the making of "insurance contracts"; and (3) whether the scope of the insurer's license includes the kind or "line" of insurance proposed to be conducted.

DEFINITION OF "DOING AN INSURANCE BUSINESS"

Usually the statutory standard for the general applicability of a particular state's regulatory scheme is whether an insurer is "doing an insurance business" (or a similar formula of words) within the geographical limits of that state. This standard is usually part of a comprehensive requirement which states that any insurer "doing an insurance business" must be licensed by the state, and to maintain the license must comply with all the requirements applicable to licensed insurers.[2] The phrase "doing an insurance business" or its equivalent is typically defined generally, and then more particularly, as including certain described activities and excluding others.

Included almost invariably are acts of making or proposing to make any "insurance contract" from inside or from outside the state, by mail or otherwise, with a resident of the state or upon "risks" located within the state.[3] Usually excluded are: (1) collecting premiums or paying claims on previously issued policies, where the insurer was licensed at the time of issuance;[4] (2) various kinds of group life and health insurance transactions based on an out-of-state master policy;[5] and (3) regardless of the location of an insured or a physical "risk" within the state, transactions based on policies primarily negotiated, issued, and delivered outside the state.[6] For example, an insurer licensed only in state X can usually issue a property or liability policy to an insured whose principal office is in state X, even though the buildings insured for fire losses or the premises insured for liability losses are located in state Y, because, legally speaking, the insurance business between the parties is being transacted or conducted only in state X.

DEFINITION OF "INSURANCE CONTRACT"

Once it is determined (or, more likely, before it is determined) that the business in question is being transacted in one state versus another, the issue may arise as to whether or not an "insurance business," or the making of an "insurance contract," is involved. A relatively detailed example of a definition of "insurance contract" is as follows:

"Insurance contract" means any agreement or other transaction whereby one party, the "insurer," is obligated to confer benefit of pecuniary value upon another party, the "insured" or "beneficiary," dependent upon the happening of a fortuitous event in which the insured or beneficiary has, or is expected to have at the time of such happening, a material interest which will be adversely affected by the happening of such event.[7]

An example of a business transaction on the borderline of insurance and noninsurance is the collision damage waiver (CDW) commonly sold by automobile rental companies. Although the courts generally have not yet determined that selling CDW is considered the making of an "insurance contract" and is therefore subject to the insurance regulatory laws, the issue has been litigated in several forums and has become the subject of specific legislation in others.[8] For example, in a 1987 California case,[9] it was held that "the presence of a small element of insurance" in a transaction whose primary purpose is the rental of a vehicle does not necessarily bring the transaction within the scope of California's insurance regulatory laws.

Similarly, in a declaratory judgment action brought by the New York Superintendent of Insurance in an effort to regulate CDW, a New York court held in 1987[10] that the sale of CDW was "merely incidental to the main contract, which is the rental of the car" and was therefore not an insurance transaction subject to regulation. This ruling was partially upset in a 1989 New York decision,[11] in which the court determined that certain other factors, such as the kind of advice offered by rental company employees and the amount of profits generated by CDW sales, may be relevant in determining whether or not an insurance transaction is present.

Another example of a borderline case is the sale of pre-paid (or "pre-need") funeral expense contracts, under which a living person pays all or part of the cost of his or her funeral to a funeral director in advance. This kind of transaction may be viewed in some jurisdictions as a form of life insurance and may be subject to regulatory controls, such as the depositing of the prepaid funds in an escrow or similar bank account.[12]

RESTRICTIONS ON NON-INSURANCE BUSINESS

Most of the financial controls imposed on insurers by law, such as investment restrictions (see Chapter 5), reserving requirements (see Chapter 5), and rate filing and approval requirements (see Chapter 7), would be virtually meaningless if insurers were free to engage in businesses other than insurance. Most states' insurance laws therefore provide that a licensed insurer may not engage in any business other than insurance or a business "necessarily or properly incidental" to insurance,[13] which may include activities such as loss adjusting, safety inspections, or premium financing.

Complementing these kinds of direct restrictions are the parts of the investment laws which prohibit insurers from investing in more than a specified percentage of the common stock of any one company or "issuer" (see Chapter 5). In this way, insurers are effectively prohibited in many instances from engaging in other businesses through the ownership of non-insurance subsidiaries.

LICENSING FOR DIFFERENT "LINES" OF BUSINESS

Licenses are usually issued with respect to one or more kinds of "lines" of insurance. These "lines" are actually subcategories within the two broad categories of life-health insurance and property-casualty insurance (see Chapter 3) into which all insurers are divided as a matter of their organizational structure. Until well into the twentieth century, non-life insurance companies were generally restricted to writing only one line, or one or more related lines, of either fire (property) or liability (casualty) insurance, so that there were virtually no "property-casualty" companies as such. These "monoline" companies tended to become affiliated with companies selling other lines and formed "groups" or "fleets" which could then provide various kinds and combinations of coverage to their customers.

The rationale for monoline companies, at least up to that time, was related to the risk of insolvency, and especially insolvencies caused by catastrophic fire losses, the idea being that the risk of insolvency should be shared by policyholders in basically the same pattern as the particular insurance risk involved. (It should be noted that the property-casualty guaranty funds, discussed in Chapter 13, are still divided into automobile, workers' compensation, and "all-other" account-categories, a partial reflection of this monoline rationale.) Another likely rationale was the thought that the management expertise of an insurer could not properly extend beyond one line of insurance.

Significant vestiges of the monoline concept remain in the areas of title insurance and financial guaranty insurance. For example, in New York, a property-casualty company must be licensed to write certain "basic kinds" or lines of insurance before it can be licensed for "non-basic" lines;[14] but no such insurer licensed to write any "basic kind" of insurance may be licensed to write title insurance,[15] so that in effect a license to write title insurance requires a monoline title insurance company which is not even considered a "property-casualty" company[16] (see Chapter 3).

The New York law, which is very detailed in this area, divides insurance into 26 lines of business, as follows:

1. life insurance;
2. annuities;
3. accident and health insurance;
4. fire insurance;
5. miscellaneous property insurance (including lightning, windstorm, flood, and the like);
6. water damage insurance (against loss due to breakage, leakage, and the like);
7. burglary and theft insurance;
8. glass insurance;
9. boiler and machinery insurance;
10. elevator insurance;
11. animal insurance;
12. collision insurance;
13. personal injury liability insurance;
14. property damage liability insurance;
15. workers' compensation and employers' liability insurance;
16. fidelity and surety insurance;
17. credit insurance;

18. title insurance;

19. motor vehicle and aircraft physical damage insurance;

20. marine and inland marine insurance;

21. marine protection and indemnity insurance;

22. residual value insurance (against loss of economic value of property);

23. mortgage guaranty insurance;

24. credit unemployment insurance;

25. financial guarantee insurance; and

26. gap insurance (covering the "gap amount" payable under a lease or loan agreement upon the total loss of the subject personal property).[17]

Of these categories, after the first three, some are designated as "basic" and others as "non-basic," with variations depending upon whether the insurer in question is a stock or mutual company. An insurer may be licensed for "non-basic" lines only if it is already licensed for a "basic" line or lines.[18]

STANDARDS FOR ISSUANCE OF LICENSES

Obtaining a license for one or more of these lines of insurance requires compliance with various statutory requirements applicable to each such line, the most important requirements being, in the case of New York, the "basic" versus "non-basic" prerequisites discussed above and the minimum capital and surplus requirements usually specified separately for certain lines. For example, a company may be required to have a surplus, or combined capital and surplus, of several million dollars to transact life insurance, whereas a few hundred thousand dollars may suffice for fire insurance.[19]

The New York law, which is fairly representative in this respect, provides that the Superintendent "may issue" a license to a domestic, foreign, or alien insurer to do the kinds of insurance business for which it is qualified under the provisions of New York law and under its charter.[20] The license must contain the name of the licensee, its home office address, the state or country under whose laws it is organized, the kinds of business it is authorized to do in New York State, and the term of the license.[21]

The Superintendent "may refuse to issue" a license or to renew a license "if in his best judgment such refusal will best promote the interests of the people of [New York State]."[22] Thus, even on the face of the statute, the amount of discretion possessed by the regulator is substantial, and the exercise of that discretion cannot easily be challenged in court.

The Superintendent is specifically authorized to refuse a license to any corporation if he or she determines after notice and a hearing that any proposed incorporator or director "has been convicted of a crime involving fraud, dishonesty, or like moral turpitude, or is an untrustworthy person."[23] No license may be granted to any corporation proposing to do business under a name identical with that of an insurer already licensed, or so similar thereto as to be "likely to deceive or mislead the public."[24]

The New York statute directs the Superintendent to do the following before licensing any domestic insurer: (1) examine the affairs of any stock corporation applying for a license to determine whether it meets the minimum capital and surplus requirements; and (2) require sworn proof from the incorporators of a mutual corporation applying for a license, to the effect that it has the minimum required surplus in cash or investments, that it has the required number and amount of applications for insurance, and that every "member" or policyholder has paid the required premium in cash and will take a policy within 60 days after a license is issued.[25]

An important aspect of the New York law is that relating to "substantial compliance." The licensing statute includes several provisions that restrict admitted insurers' activities in other states. The most general of these is a provision which states that, except as specifically provided otherwise in the Insurance Law, no foreign or alien insurer shall be licensed or have its license renewed if it fails to "comply substantially with any requirement or limitation of [the Insurance Law], applicable to similar domestic insurers hereafter to be organized, which in the judgment of the superintendent is reasonably necessary to protect the interests of the people of this state."[26]

Considering the fact that New York's regulatory requirements on the whole are probably the most rigorous in the nation, these provisions have the so-called "extra-territorial" effect of extending the application of New York law to many insurers' activities in other states. These provisions also lead many other insurers to conclude that, due to the nature of their business, they should not or cannot become licensed in New York.

Some states require, either by statute or as a matter of insurance department policy, that an insurer seeking a license for a particular line of business have experience in that line of business in another state or states for a certain period of time, such as three years or five years. These requirements, commonly referred to as "seasoning" requirements, may be inapplicable if an insurer is a member of a holding company group (see Chapter 11) in which another member has the required experience.

"RETALIATORY" REQUIREMENTS

As a consequence of the individual states' power to enact non-uniform insurance licensing laws, and each state's interest in protecting its own domestic companies, most states have enacted "retaliatory" licensing provisions.[27] These provisions basically state that if domestic insurers of state X are subjected in state Z to any fees or requirements in excess of what state X imposes on state Z's domestic companies, then the requirements of state Z will be applied by state X to state Z's companies. For example, if state Z imposes a $5,000 license application fee on state X's domestic companies, state X will also impose a $5,000 fee on any of state Z's companies applying for a license (even if state X normally charges only $500 for such an application).

Section 1112 of the New York Insurance Law contains comprehensive retaliatory provisions regarding taxes, fines, penalties, license fees, and security deposit requirements of other states. They extend to other states' requirements applicable to agents and brokers as well as insurers.

DURATION, REVOCATION, AND SUSPENSION OF LICENSES

Although requirements vary among the states, in New York a license for a domestic company is for an indefinite term and ends only when the corporate existence ends. Foreign and alien insurer's licenses expire each June 30 following the date of issuance or renewal, but may be renewed upon the filing of the annual statement (see Chapter 5).[28] A license may be revoked if the Superintendent determines after notice and a hearing that the insurer has violated any provision of the Insurance Law and "such revocation is reasonably necessary to protect the interests of the people of this state".[29] Most other states have similar provisions, including the "due process" requirements of notice and a hearing.[30] The New York law also provides that a license may be reinstated in the Superintendent's discretion if he or she finds that the grounds for revocation no longer exist.[31]

SURRENDER OF LICENSES; PLANS OF WITHDRAWAL

Most states' insurance laws include provisions that prevent insurers from withdrawing or "leaving the marketplace" under circumstances which would leave policyholders without necessary coverage or with a reduced measure of security, or which would otherwise be disruptive. For example, New York requires any insurer that "proposes to cease to maintain its existing licensing status" to submit to the Superintendent a plan to protect the interests of New York residents, including procedures for meeting all contractual (i.e., policy) and statutory obligations and providing security for such obligations in the event of a subsequent insolvency.[32] The plan must comply with regulations promulgated by the Superintendent and must be approved by the Superintendent in advance of the proposed action.[33]

NOTES

1. See, e.g., *Allgeyer v. Louisiana*, 165 U.S. 578 (1896).
2. See N.Y. Ins. Law Sec. 1102(a).
3. *Id.* Sec. 1101(b)(1).
4. *Id.* Subsection (b)(2)(C).

5. *Id.* Subsection (b)(2)(B).

6. *Id.* Subsection (b)(2)(E).

7. *Id.* Subsection (a)(1).

8. See generally, Lentz, "The Collision Damage Waiver," *Federation of Insurance & Corporate Counsel Quarterly*, Fall 1989.

9. *Truta v. Avis Rent-a-Car Corp.*, 238 Cal. Rptr. 806 (1987).

10. *Hertz Corp. v. Corcoran*, 520 N.Y.S.2d 700 (1987).

11. *Hertz Corp. v. Corcoran*, 539 N.Y.S.2d 258 (1989).

12. See, e.g., Fla. Ins. Code Sec. 639.055 et seq.

13. N.Y. Ins. Law Sec. 1113(a).

14. *Id.* Sec. 4101 et seq.

15. *Id.* Sec. 4102(c).

16. *Id.* Sec. 6401 et seq.

17. *Id.* Sec. 1113(a).

18. *Id.* Sec. 4102(b).

19. Compare N.Y. Ins. Law Secs. 4202(a) and 4103(a).

20. N.Y. Ins. Law Sec. 1102(d).

21. *Id.*

22. *Id.*

23. N.Y. Ins. Law Sec. 1102(e)(2).

24. *Id.* Subsection (g)(1).

25. *Id.* Subsection (e)(1).

26. N.Y. Ins. Law Sec. 1106(e).

27. *Id.* Sec. 1112(a).

28. *Id.* Sec. 1103.

29. *Id.* Sec. 1104(a).

30. Ill. Ins. Code Sec. 119(2).

31. N.Y. Ins. Law Sec. 1104(a).

32. *Id.* Sec. 1105.

33. *Id.*

5

Insurers' Assets, Reserves, and Investments

STATUTORY ACCOUNTING PRINCIPLES (SAP) VERSUS GENERALLY ACCEPTED ACCOUNTING PRINCIPLES (GAAP)

The principles of accounting that apply to most businesses are referred to as "generally accepted accounting principles," or GAAP. With respect to the statutory regulation of insurance companies, however, GAAP accounting is not used because different principles are required by statute. These statutory principles are, predictably, referred to as "SAP," or statutory accounting principles. (Although GAAP is usually pronounced as "gap," SAP is not normally pronounced as "sap." It is customary to talk about "gap" versus "statutory" accounting, or results measured on a "gap" basis versus a "statutory" basis.) GAAP and SAP are not completely different methods of accounting, but there are many significant differences that can make the "bottom line" change appreciably. Another set of accounting principles, those of tax accounting, apply in various ways to the federal income taxation of insurance companies (see Chapter 16).

Because the maintenance of solvency is the primary goal of insurance regulation, and because the solvency of any enterprise is determined primarily by comparing assets and liabilities, insurers' balance sheets and related financial statements are a primary subject of regulatory concern. (The formal requirements pertaining to the preparation and filing of "annual statements" with the regulators are discussed in Chapter 6.) The legal solvency of most business enterprises is usually determined under two sets of criteria: (1) the "balance-sheet test" of solvency, which requires that assets be at least equal to liabilities; and (2) the "liquidity test," which requires that there be sufficient "liquid" assets readily convertible into money to pay all obligations as they become due. The various states' insurance regulatory laws may embody either or both of these tests, or variations of them.

The basic underlying premises of the laws governing "admitted assets," reserves, and insurer investments are: (1) that assets used to counterbalance liabilities must be secure, diversified, and conservatively valued; and (2) that all fixed and contingent liabilities, such as anticipated claims and other future obligations, must be recognized as such, with a reasonable degree of accuracy as to their amounts.

The liability side of an insurer's balance sheet is quite different from that of other kinds of businesses because most of what appears there is only an estimate. These estimates of liabilities to policyholders and beneficiaries are called "reserves," and despite the connotations of that term, they are not to be confused with the assets which are their counterparts on the other side of the balance sheet.

LIFE INSURANCE RESERVES

The different nature of policy reserves for life insurers as compared with property-casualty insurers illustrates the dissimilarity between the two kinds of business. Life insurance reserves usually consist mostly of "policy reserves," which may be loosely defined as the present value of future policy benefits minus the present value of future premium considerations, if any, for those same benefits.[1] Present value is synonymous with discounted value, and means the amount which, with interest added and compounded an assumed rate, will equal a larger given amount at a certain time in the future.

The definition of policy reserves therefore contemplates a relatively long-term contractual relationship prior to the maturity of the obligation (normally a death claim) as well as the relative certainty of its eventual maturity (because every insured ultimately dies). In other words, at least with respect to the classic "ordinary life" policy where fixed premiums are payable for life and coverage is guaranteed for life, both the eventual claim obligation of the insurer, and the interim periodic premium obligation of the policyholder, are assumed.

Many states have enacted versions of the NAIC'S Model "Standard Valuation Law," which includes mandatory formulas for determining the proper amount of reserves for different kinds of life insurance and annuity contracts. (See the columns labeled "Std. Valuation Law" in Appendix 3.) These laws usually prescribe the use of certain mortality tables, such as the 1980 Commissioners Standard Ordinary Mortality Table (the "1980 CSO Table"), certain assumed rates of interest, and certain actuarial methods of computation, such as the "net level premium method."

Until 1992, life insurers were required to establish a "Mandatory Securities Valuation Reserve" as an additional liability on their balance sheets, in order to allow for possible adverse fluctuations in the value of publicly traded securities held by them as investments. (The MSVR has been phased out and replaced by other valuation reserves, as discussed in "Valuation of Securities," below). Life insurers may also carry annuity reserves[2] which represent the amount of money, held at interest, which will be sufficient to pay periodic pension or other annuity benefits during certain periods, or for the entire lifetime of some annuitants. These reserves may relate to individual or group annuity contracts (see Chapter 8).

PROPERTY-CASUALTY RESERVES

In contrast, there are usually no "policy reserves" on the property-casualty insurer's balance sheet. Instead, there are two other kinds of reserves: loss reserves and unearned premium reserves. Loss reserves relate primarily to incurred losses (that is, accidents, or other events giving rise to liability, that have already happened), and they include the following: (1) the estimated value of known (or "reported"), incurred claims, whether discounted or not; (2) the estimated loss adjustment expenses (including attorneys' fees) associated with those claims; and (3) a provision for losses "incurred but not reported" (usually called "IBNR").[3]

For example, assuming that an automobile accident happened on December 31, 1995 and was reported and investigated immediately, an insurer might establish on its 1995 year-end balance sheet a reported loss reserve of $50,000 for personal injury to the driver of the automobile, and a loss adjustment reserve of $10,000 for the expected cost of investigation and litigation. Based on other late-December accidents in the aggregate, the details of which are largely or entirely unknown, the insurer might also set up (on the 1995 balance sheet) a proportionate IBNR reserve to reflect the claims of persons injured or property damaged in other accidents which could be asserted or "reported" to the insurer in early 1996 or later, but which were "incurred" in (i.e., on the basis of accidents which happened in) 1995. IBNR reserves are especially important in reserving for lines of business like medical malpractice, where many losses are not reported (or even known) for months or years after they are incurred.

The adequacy of loss reserves, including IBNR, is a subject of great concern among regulators and within the industry generally, because many property-casualty insurer insolvencies have been caused at least in part by "under-reserving," i.e., the negligent or intentional underestimation of future loss payments. In recent years, insurers have been required to have a qualified actuary certify periodically that their reserves are reasonably accurate and adequate (see Chapter 6).

Unearned premium reserves represent the liability of a property-casualty insurer to refund a proportionate part of premiums paid in advance, in the event of mid-term cancellation of a policy by the insurer or the insured.[4] For example, a one-year policy issued on January 1 for a premium of $1,000 will initially give rise to an unearned premium reserve of approximately $1,000; that reserve will decline to approximately $500 by June 30, and to zero by December 31.

Under statutory accounting principles, and contrary to what GAAP accounting would dictate, the full amount of unearned premium reserve on a new policy must be accounted for as a liability, without any deduction for the broker's or other sales representative's commission (even though a proportionate part of the commission must be repaid if the policy is cancelled). This requirement effectively limits the amount of new business a property-casualty insurer can write, since the insurer's surplus is reduced by the amount of commissions paid.[5]

ADMITTED ASSETS AND PERMISSIBLE INVESTMENTS

Because solvency depends upon the certainty that an insurer's assets will be adequate to pay all of its future liabilities in a timely manner, the kinds of assets that can legally be used for investment purposes, and to determine an insurer's "statutory" financial condition, are limited. The somewhat archaic term of art used to describe assets that can be used in this way is "admitted assets,"[6] that is, assets that the regulator will allow or "admit" under applicable law. The underlying premise is that such assets must be reasonably secure, both as to recovery of the amount invested and as to the rate of return, over a substantial period of time.

To put it differently, such assets must be held largely in the form of investments that are not, on the whole, speculative. In some states, such as New York, the law defines "admitted assets" as including permitted investments, a category which is then further defined.[7] In other states, such as New Jersey,[8] the law simply states that an insurer may invest its capital, surplus, and other funds only in certain permitted investments, as specified therein. The practical effect of both kinds of law is very much the same.

Although the investment laws are complex (especially in the case of New York) and varied, they basically require a very large part of insurers' assets to be invested in government and corporate bonds or other debt obligations, common and preferred stock, real estate, and mortgages on real estate.[9] Admitted assets usually do not include such items as good will, trade names, furniture, or fixtures.[10] Non-income producing investments such as precious metals are generally not permitted, but options and futures contracts may be allowed, subject to stringent limitations.

In general, assets in the form of debt obligations must be adequately secured by some specific collateral, such as real estate, plant and equipment, inventory, or other tangible assets.[11] (The term "bond," when applied to corporate obligations, usually implies that there is such underlying collateral, whereas terms like "note" or "debenture" imply that there is not.) Nevertheless, unsecured notes or debentures may qualify under many laws as admitted assets if their issuers have a substantial record of earnings and financial strength.[12]

"Junk bonds" is the colloquial name for unsecured, subordinated debentures, which are financial obligations that will be paid only after most other corporate debts and obligations. Depending upon the issuer, such bonds may or may not be eligible for treatment as admitted assets. New York has imposed percentage limitations on junk bond holdings (referred to as "medium grade" and "lower grade" obligations) by regulation since 1987.[13]

A unique form of asset held by life insurance companies is the aggregate value of outstanding policy loans.[14] Policyholders who own cash value life insurance policies may "borrow" or receive advances against the cash value without surrendering their policies for cancellation. Because the receivables represented by these loans are fully secured (or offset) by the policies' cash values, they are usually considered admitted assets, the same as other adequately secured obligations. Normally the amount of a policy loan on any particular policy is limited to the individual policy reserve, which is part of the insurer's aggregate policy reserves. The "assets" comprised of policy loan receivables can therefore be viewed from a different perspective as reductions in policy reserves.

As of 1995, approximately 76 percent of property-casualty insurers' assets and 60 percent of life insurers' assets were invested in government securities and corporate bonds.[15] Government bonds normally are the most secure investment available, especially if they are "general revenue" obligations or are supported by the "full faith and credit" of the United States or other issuer, and they invariably qualify as permitted investments.[16] Canadian government securities are frequently given the same status as obligations of the United States and its political subdivisions.[17]

Most investment laws also include a so-called "leeway" or "basket" provision, which allows insurers to invest a small portion of their assets, such as 5 percent, in any medium, without regard to the limitations otherwise imposed by the law.[18] In some states, there are further percentage sublimits on particular investments within the "basket."

VALUATION OF SECURITIES

A rather unique aspect of insurance investment activity and regulation is the "amortization" method of valuation of securities—specifically bonds and other fixed-income obligations. Because neither the liquidity nor the inherent value of a security is fully meaningful by itself, in general, bonds must be valued for SAP purposes, not based on their purchase price or their current market value, but instead on the basis of their "amortized value," which may be defined as follows: (1) for bonds purchased at par value (face amount), the par value; and (2) for bonds purchased above or below par value, and amount which will equal par value at the maturity date of the bond, assuming that interest is earned to maturity at the initial rate of yield.[19]

Common stock, however, is normally valued at market value,[20] at least partly because it has no ultimate, guaranteed maturity value. Since stocks generally are more speculative investments than bonds, the market-value method of valuation tends to emphasize short-term liquidity rather than long-term stability and has the effect of discouraging investments in stock for many insurers. Preferred stock is usually valued at cost, and in this respect it is treated more like bonds and other fixed-income investments.

As mentioned above, until 1992, life insurers were required to establish a Mandatory Securities Valuation Reserve (MSVR) to provide a buffer for fluctuations in the value of securities held as investments.[21] The calculation of the amount of this reserve was a very technical process based upon a differentiation between realized and unrealized capital gains as applied to common stock, preferred stock, and bonds.[22] The MSVR has now been replaced by the Asset Valuation Reserve (AVR), which measures changes caused by fluctuating creditworthiness, and the Interest Maintenance Reserve (IMR), which takes into account realized capital gains and losses caused by interest rate changes. The AVR covers real estate and mortgages as well as securities, and the IMR covers government as well as corporate obligations.

The valuation of many publicly traded securities is covered by the NAIC's Securities Valuation Manual, and many states require the values determined in accordance with the Manual to be used on insurers' annual statements. The Manual also specifies which bonds are eligible for amortization and which are to be valued otherwise (for example, based on their market value). The NAIC maintains an office in New York City, called the Securities Valuation Office, in connection with the preparation and use of the Manual.

DIVERSIFICATION AND BOARD APPROVAL OF INVESTMENTS

Another important investment requirement is diversification. The diversification rule (which also applies in other legal contexts, such as trusts and estates) provides that investments should not be unduly concentrated in any one medium, so that the risk of loss due to particular bad investments can be minimized. Typically the applicable state's insurance law will provide that no more than a certain percentage (such as 10 percent) of admitted assets of an insurer may be invested in any one parcel of real property, or in the debt securities (bonds or debentures) of any one issuer.[23] It may also impose limitations on the percentage of any issuer's preferred or common shares, or a class thereof, which an insurer may hold.[24]

Investments may be routinely acquired and disposed of under the supervision of an insurer's officers, in their discretion. Under many states' laws, however, each investment decision must be reviewed and approved or "ratified" after the fact by the board of directors at its next meeting.[25]

DIVIDENDS AND SURPLUS

Like any other business entity, a regulated insurance company has an entry on its balance sheet for "surplus," also known as retained earnings. Sometimes an insurer's surplus is referred to as "policyholders' surplus" whether or not the insurer is a mutual company, because the surplus account is viewed as an extra measure of protection for policyholders, above and beyond the insurer's statutory reserve liabilities. In any event, surplus can also be viewed as an amount of "owners' equity" which is at risk if the insurer's reserves ever prove to be inadequate.

Both stock and mutual companies may pay dividends out of surplus. A stock company may pay either stock dividends to its shareholders (the same as any business corporation) or policy dividends to its policyholders, or both. A mutual company, by its nature, can pay only policyholder dividends (see Chapter 2). Regulatory approval may be required for payment of stock dividends or policyholder dividends, either by stock or mutual companies.[26] The usual criterion for approval of policy dividends is that they be fair and equitable, and not unfairly discriminatory.[27] Generally this means that dividends must be apportioned to different classifications of policies based upon the amount of profits attributable to those classifications. Dividends may be paid out of currently earned surplus, or in some cases out of accumulated surplus.

Life insurance companies are affirmatively required under some states' laws to calculate and distribute a portion of their surplus periodically in the form of dividends on all "participating" policies, that is, those which provide specifically for the payment of annual dividends.[28] Such a requirement may be coupled with a limitation on the amount of surplus a life insurer may accumulate.[29] Traditionally, dividends have been a non-guaranteed but generally reliable factor in the pricing of life insurance, since many policies are sold on the basis of "illustrations" of what their net cost will be if dividends continue to be paid according to recent patterns.

Under New York law, life insurers are also subject to detailed limitations on the amount of new life and annuity business they can write,[30] and on the amount of expenses they can incur for sales commissions and related matters.[31] New York also has extensive regulations regarding reimbursement of agency expenses,[32] the payment of additional commissions to new general agents,[33] and the payment of training allowances to new soliciting agents.[34] Because of these restrictions, many life insurance companies have separate, New York-only subsidiaries.

REINSURANCE CEDED AND ASSUMED

Because almost all insurers purchase reinsurance to protect themselves from disastrous claims, the value of reinsurance as an asset is an important part of the regulatory picture. Reinsurance can be defined as the transfer, by agreement, of all or part of the risks underwritten by one insurer (the "ceding" company) to another insurer (the "assuming" company or reinsurer). Many insurers assume other companies' risks by reinsurance; most insurers cede part of their risks to other companies by reinsurance. Some insurers called "professional reinsurers" engage only in the business of reinsurance.

For most lines of insurance, insurers are prohibited by statute in most states from permanently accepting or "retaining" more than certain specified amounts of risk, such as one-tenth of the amount of their surplus on any one property or liability risk,[35] so if they insure any risks in excess of these amounts they are legally required to obtain reinsurance for the excess portion. In addition, apart from legal requirements, most insurers (except perhaps the very largest companies) find it prudent to obtain reinsurance on certain risks or certain kinds of business, in order to minimize the effect of catastrophic losses, to stabilize their operating results, and in some cases to "leverage" or increase the amount of direct insurance they can write.

Because reinsurance is a normal and necessary part of most companies' operations, statutory accounting principles ordinarily allow for the recognition of "reinsurance recoverable" as an asset (or a reduction in reserve liabilities) on a ceding company's books and of "reinsurance assumed" as a liability on the reinsurer's books.[36] The amounts of these entries depend on the terms of the applicable reinsurance agreements or "treaties," but in general they represent a proportionate amount of the corresponding reserves which would normally be held by the ceding company in the absence of reinsurance. Amounts of money or other assets based upon these transferred liabilities are normally transferred by the ceding company to the reinsurer pursuant to the terms of the reinsurance agreement.

Because the adequacy of the reserves (and the quality of the corresponding assets) held by reinsurers is vital to the ceding company's solvency, the value of its reinsurance recoverable is normally recognized by the regulator only if the reinsurer is licensed in the regulator's state or otherwise approved as an "accredited" foreign or alien insurer.[37] Listings of such accredited reinsurers are sometimes promulgated by regulation or otherwise made public in many states. If a foreign or alien reinsurer is not "accredited," the reinsurer must ordinarily provide (1) a deposit of cash or securities with the ceding company, (2) an amount of cash or securities in trust with a domestic bank or other suitable trustee, or (3) an irrevocable letter of credit issued by an acceptable bank to secure the reinsurer's obligations.[38]

Reinsurance ceded and assumed is accounted for and reported on Schedule F of the standard property-casualty annual statement, and on Schedule S of the standard life company statement (see Chapter 6). Regulation of reinsurance is more fully discussed in Chapter 14.

STATUTORY DEPOSITS OF SECURITIES

As part of the licensing process, including the periodic renewal of insurers' licenses where applicable, many states require insurers to deposit bonds or other securities with the insurance regulator, or with a custodian designated by the regulator.[39] The primary purpose of these requirements is to guarantee that, in the event the insurer becomes insolvent, there will be a source of funds for payment of claims and other obligations within the state. The amount of the deposit required is usually related to the minimum capital and surplus required of the insurer for the lines of insurance involved. These deposited securities are still considered the property of the insurer for most purposes, and they are normally part of its admitted assets. They may be exchanged for other eligible securities from time to time, and the interest or other income on them is normally payable to the insurer.

"SEPARATE ACCOUNTS" FOR VARIABLE AND OTHER CONTRACTS

Finally, the laws of many states allow life insurers to create "separate accounts," not subject to the usual rules regarding investments, primarily for pension assets and variable life and annuity products. These laws reflect the passing of the investment risk from the insurer to the policyholders in question. For example, if the amount of life insurance payable on the death of a particular policyholder is tied to the value of a portfolio of speculative common stocks, the insurer bears some mortality risk but no appreciable investment risk. In such cases, it is appropriate to recognize for accounting purposes that the insurer's overall financial condition is not affected by this investment risk.

Most of these laws provide that: (1) assets comprising separate accounts are to be valued at their market value; (2) income, gains, and losses (whether realized or not) are to be charged to the applicable account (i.e., segregated) without regard to any other income, gains, or losses of the insurer; and (3) the usual investment limitation rules do not apply to separate accounts.[40]

NOTES

1. See N.Y. Ins. Law Sec. 1304.
2. *Id.* Subsection (a).
3. See N.Y. Ins. Law Sec. 1303.
4. *Id.* Sec. 1305.
5. S. Mooney and L. Cohen, *Basic Concepts of Accounting and Taxation of Property/ Casualty Insurance Companies* (New York: Insurance Information Institute Press, 1991), p. 22.
6. *Id.* Sec. 1301.
7. *Id.* Sec. 1401 et seq.
8. N.J.S.A. 17:24–1.
9. See N.Y. Ins. Law Sec. 1404.
10. *Id.* Sec. 1302.
11. *Id.* Sec. 1404(a)(2)(A).
12. *Id.* Subsection (a)(2)(B)–(D).
13. N.Y. Insurance Dept. Regulation 130.
14. See N.Y. Ins. Law. Sec. 1406.
15. *1997 Property-Casualty Fact Book* (Insurance Information Institute, 1997), p. 20;

1996 Life Insurance Fact Book (Washington, D.C.: American Council of Life Insurance, 1996), pp. 84–85.

16. See, e.g., N.Y. Ins. Law Sec. 1404(a)(1).

17. *Id.* Subsection (a)(8).

18. *Id.* Subsection (b).

19. See N.Y. Ins. Law Sec. 1414(a).

20. *Id.* Subsection (b).

21. Black and Skipper, *Life Insurance* (Englewood Cliffs, N.J.: Prentice Hall, 12th ed., 1994), pp. 918–919.

22. *Id.*

23. See N.Y. Ins. Law Secs. 1404(a)(7)(F) and 1404(a)(2)(H).

24. *Id.* Secs. 1404(a)(3)(B) and 1404(a)(13)(B).

25. *Id.* Sec. 1411(a).

26. *Id.* Secs. 4207(a) (stock life companies) and 4114 (mutual property-casualty companies).

27. *Id.* Sec. 4114.

28. *Id.* Sec. 4231.

29. *Id.* Sec. 4219.

30. *Id.* Sec. 4227.

31. *Id.* Sec. 4228.

32. N.Y. Ins. Dept. Regulation 49.

33. N.Y. Ins. Dept. Regulation 50.

34. *Id.*

35. See, e.g., N.Y. Ins. Law Sec. 1115.

36. *Id.* Secs. 1301(a)(14) and 1308; and Ill. Ins. Code Sec. 173.

37. *Id.* Secs. 1301(a)(14) and 107(a)(2); and Ill. Ins. Code Sec. 173.1(1).

38. See, e.g., Ill. Ins. Code Sec. 173.1(2).

39. See N.Y. Ins. Law Secs. 1314 et seq. (general); 4104 (property-casualty); and 4206 (life).

40. *Id.* Sec. 4240(a)(1), (2), and (7).

6

Annual Statements and Periodic Examinations

STANDARD FORM OF ANNUAL STATEMENT; FILING REQUIREMENTS

Probably the single most important requirement in insurance regulation is that relating to an insurer's annual statement, which is a financial report to the insurance departments of the states where the insurer is authorized to do business. The form of the annual statement is mostly standardized by agreement among the regulators under the auspices of the National Association of Insurance Commissioners (NAIC). It is often referred to as the "Convention Blank," because the NAIC was known as the National Convention of Insurance Commissioners until 1935. Each state's insurance law requires licensed insurers to complete and file such a report annually, usually by the first day of March, on the basis of their financial condition as of the preceding December 31. (See the columns labeled "Annual Statements" in Appendix 3.)

The purpose of the annual statement is full disclosure of the insurer's financial condition to regulators and the public, including all existing and potential policyholders, agents and brokers, ceding and assuming reinsurers, and other interested persons. (Of course, there are additional disclosure requirements under the securities laws for publicly owned insurance companies and insurance holding companies.) Annual statements, prepared in accordance with statutory accounting principles (see Chapter 5), are submitted to regulators for scrutiny, and at the same time they become public documents which open a large part of insurers' internal operations and external relationships to public view.

PROPERTY-CASUALTY INSURERS: CONTENTS OF STATEMENTS

The contents of the standard property-casualty statement (sometimes called the "Yellow Book") include:

1. a year-end balance sheet, also called a statement of Assets, Liabilities, Surplus and Other Funds;

2. an Underwriting and Investment Exhibit, which includes a Statement of Income; a Cash Flow statement; summaries of Interest, Dividends, and Real Estate Income; Capital Gains and Losses on Investments; Premiums Earned, Losses Paid and Incurred, Unpaid Losses and Adjustment Expenses; and a listing of general Expenses;

3. exhibits showing an analysis of admitted and non-admitted assets;

4. general interrogatories (i.e., questions) and responses from the insurer concerning various kinds of investments and other transactions of the company;

5. a schedule of statutory deposits held by insurance regulatory authorities;

6. a five-year historical analysis of premiums, losses, and expenses;

7. Schedules A through Y, which include detailed information about assets and investments bought, sold, and held at year-end; reinsurance transactions; and losses and loss expenses over a ten-year period (see Table 6.1); and

8. an organizational chart or similar display showing the relationships between the insurer and all of its affiliates and subsidiaries.

LIFE-HEALTH INSURERS: CONTENTS OF STATEMENTS

The contents of the standard life-health company statement (sometimes called the "Blue Book") include the following:

1. a statement of assets, liabilities, surplus and other funds;

2. a Summary of Operations, Capital and Surplus Account, Cash Flow, and Analysis of Operations by Line of Business;

3. Exhibits 1 through 14, which include a great amount of detailed information about premiums, dividends, investment results, claims, and reserves (see Table 6.2);

4. Schedules A through Y, which are detailed summaries of assets and investments bought, sold, and held at year-end, and of reinsurance transactions (see Table 6.2);

5. if applicable, a Separate Account Statement and/or Variable Life Insurance Separate Account Statement (see Chapter 5); and

6. an organizational chart or similar display showing the relationships between the insurer and its affiliates and subsidiaries.

Table 6.1
Contents of Property-Casualty Company Annual Statement

Assets
Liabilities, Surplus and Other Funds
Statement of Income and Capital & Surplus Account
Cash Flow
Underwriting and Investment Exhibit
      Part 1 -- Interest, Dividends and Real Estate Income
      Part 1A -- Capital Gains and Losses on Investments
      Part 2 -- Premiums Earned
      Part 2A -- Recapitulation of All Premiums
      Part 2B -- Premiums Written
      Part 3 -- Losses Paid and Incurred
      Part 3A -- Unpaid Losses and Loss Adjustment Expenses
      Part 4 -- Expenses
Exhibit 1 -- Analysis of Assets
Exhibit 2 -- Analysis of Non-Admitted Assets
Exhibit 3 -- Reconciliation of Ledger Assets
Direct Business in the State of ...
Medicare Supplement Insurance Experience Exhibit
General Interrogatories
Notes to Financial Statements
Schedule of Special Deposits
Five-year Historical Data
Schedule A (Real Estate)*
Schedule B (Long-Term Mortgages; Other Long Term Invested Assets)*
Schedule C (Long-Term Collateral Loans)*
Schedule D (Bonds; Preferred and Common Stocks)*
Schedule DA (Short-Term Investments)*
Schedule DB (Derivative Instruments; Options, Caps and Floors;
      Collar, Swap and Forward Agreements; Futures Contracts)*
Schedule DC (Insurance Futures and Insurance Futures Options)*
Schedule F (Reinsurance)*
Schedule H (Accident and Health Exhibit)*
Schedule M (Salaries of Officers and Directors; Payments to Various
      Organizations)*
Schedule N -- Cash
Schedule P -- Analysis of Losses and Loss Expenses*
Schedule X -- Unlisted Assets
Schedule Y -- Information Concerning Activities of Insurer Members of
      a Holding Company Group
Schedule Y -- Part 2 -- Summary of Insurer's Transactions with Any
      Affiliates
Schedule T -- Exhibit of Premiums Written Allocated by States and Territories

(*Note: these Schedules include various component Parts and Sections
not fully listed here.)

Table 6.2
Contents of Life-Health Company Annual Statement

Assets
Liabilities, Surplus and Other Funds
Summary of Operations (Excluding Unrealized Capital Gains and Losses)
Capital and Surplus Account
Cash Flow
Analysis of Operations by Lines of Business
Analysis of Increase in Reserves and Deposit Funds During the Year
Exhibit 1 -- Part 1 -- Premiums and Annuity Considerations
Exhibit 1 -- Part 2 -- Dividends and Coupons Applied, Reinsurance
      Commissions and Expense Allowances and Commissions Incurred
Exhibit 2 -- Net Investment Income
Exhibit 3 -- Realized Capital Gains and (Losses) on Investments
Exhibit 4 -- Unrealized Capital Gains and (Losses) on Investments
Exhibit 5 -- General Expenses
Exhibit 6 -- Taxes, Licenses & Fees
Exhibit 7 -- Dividends and Coupons to Policyholders
Exhibit 8 -- Aggregate Reserve for Life Policies and Contracts
Exhibit 8 -- Question 3
Exhibit 8A -- Changes in Bases of Valuation During the Year
Exhibit 9 -- Aggregate Reserve for Accident and Health Policies
Exhibit 10 -- Deposit Funds and Other Liabilities Without Life or Disability
      Contingencies
Exhibit 11 -- Policy and Contract Claims -- Part 1 -- Liability End of Current
      Year
Exhibit 11 -- Policy and Contract Claims -- Part 2 -- Incurred During the Year
Exhibit 12 -- Reconciliation of Ledger Assets
Exhibit 13 -- Assets
Exhibit 14 -- Analysis of Nonadmitted Assets and Related Items
State page
Medicare Supplement Insurance Experience Exhibit
Five-Year Historical Data
Exhibit of Life Insurance
Exhibit of Number of Policies, Contracts, etc.
General Interrogatories
Notes to Financial Statements
Schedule of Special Deposits
Schedule A (Real Estate)*
Schedule B (Mortgages)*
Schedule C (Long-Term Collateral Loans)*
Schedule D (Bonds)*
Schedule DA (Short-Term Investments)*
Schedule DB (Derivative Instruments; Options, Caps and Floors;
      Collar, Swap and Forward Agreements; Futures Contracts)*
Schedule DC (Insurance Futures and Insurance Futures Options)*
Schedule E -- Cash
Schedule F -- Death Claims Resisted or Compromised
Schedule H -- Accident and Health Exhibit

Table 6.2 Continued

Schedule M -- Disclosure of Dividend Practices
Schedule O -- Development of Incurred Losses
Schedule S -- Reinsurance*
Schedule X -- Unlisted Assets
Schedule Y -- Information Concerning Activities of Insurer Members of a
    Holding Company Group
Schedule Y -- Part 2 -- Summary of Insurer's Transactions with Any Affiliates
Schedule T -- Premium and Annuity Considerations Allocated by States and
    Territories
Long Term Care Experience Reporting Forms

(*Note: these Schedules include various component Parts and Sections
not fully listed here.)

CERTIFICATION OF ANNUAL STATEMENTS

Virtually all states require annual statements to be certified as accurate by officers of the insurer (usually the president and secretary).[1] A substantial number of states also require that independent accountants provide a certification to the effect that the statement meets certain criteria of financial reporting.[2] Independent certification by an accounting firm is intended to prevent or detect insolvency, since financial statements prepared entirely by the insurer's officers and other "insiders" may be biased or otherwise inaccurate, especially in the case of financially weak companies.

EXAMINATIONS AND THE "ZONE SYSTEM"

Most state laws provide that the regulator may examine a licensed insurer as often as he or she deems it necessary, and that the regulator is obligated to examine each insurer no less often than every three or five years.[3] (The examination requirements of the various states are identified in the columns labeled "Examinations" in Appendix 3.) Virtually every state insurance department employs full-time examiners who specialize in conducting company examinations and preparing reports of their findings.

Each financial examination (see below) ordinarily focuses on the insurer's condition as of December 31 of a particular year, so that the examiners taking part in an examination are not primarily concerned with the insurer's current condition, but instead are engaged in reconstructing and verifying a past state of affairs. For example, an examination being conducted in the middle of 1995 may relate to the applicable insurer's assets, investments, reserves, and other aspects of its condition as of December 31, 1993.

To prevent unnecessary duplication of efforts, the laws of many states also provide that, instead of making a direct examination of a licensed insurer, a regulator may accept the report of the insurance department of another state where the insurer is licensed.[4] This flexibility of the examination requirements makes possible the "Zone System" of examinations sponsored by the NAIC. Under this system, representatives of insurance departments from four different geographical zones, each consisting of several states (see Table 6.3), form teams to examine insurers and prepare reports of their examinations, on behalf of all the regulators in the various zones. In general, any company licensed in more than one zone, or in more than three states within one zone, is likely to be subject to a zone examination.

Examinations are divided into "financial condition" and "market conduct" examinations, although both kinds of examination may take place simultaneously. Financial condition examinations involve the following kinds of inquiry: (1) the history of the company, its management and control, and its records generally; (2) the company's insurance, bonding, and pension plans; (3) the company's territory, method of operation, underwriting practices, and the geographical mix of its business; and (4) the company's underwriting experience, reinsurance program, and financial statements, including assets, investments, and surplus position.[5] Financial examinations may result in material revisions of some insurers' SAP financials, and may even lead to findings of insolvency in extreme cases.

In contrast, market conduct examinations concern the following: (1) methods of sales and advertising, including compliance with applicable regulations; (2) underwriting, including compliance with statutory and other restrictions on discrimination and anti-competitive practices; (3) rating practices, particularly compliance with rate and form filing and approval requirements; (4) claim practices; and (5) handling of complaints from policyholders and others.[6] Market conduct examinations frequently result in monetary fines being imposed upon insurers for intentional or unintentional violations, such as the use of unapproved rates, or unreasonable delays in making claim payments.

Most states' statutes provide that the expenses of conducting an examination, including personnel expenses, shall be borne by the insurer in question.[7] Some statutes provide in some detail for the treatment of certain expenses, such as travel and living expenses.[8]

REPORTS ON EXAMINATIONS

Most states' statutes also direct the regulator to prepare a written report following the examination of an insurer, and to submit the report to the insurer's management for comments or corrections before the report becomes final and is made available for public inspection.[9] The insurer may have a right to a hearing on any disputed matters contained in the report.[10] Some states also require that each director of the insurer receive and acknowledge a copy of the report.[11] The evident purpose of such provisions is to ensure that the contents of the report are accurate and that those ultimately responsible for the insurer's operations and financial condition are made aware of the contents.

Table 6.3
NAIC Zone System

Northeastern Zone (Zone I)

Connecticut	New Jersey
Delaware	New York
District of Columbia	Pennsylvania
Maine	Rhode Island
Maryland	Vermont
Massachusetts	Virgin Islands
New Hampshire	

Southeastern Zone (Zone II)

Alabama	North Carolina
Arkansas	Puerto Rico
Florida	South Carolina
Georgia	Tennessee
Kentucky	Virginia
Louisiana	West Virginia
Mississippi	

Midwestern Zone (Zone III)

Iowa	Nebraska
Illinois	North Dakota
Indiana	Ohio
Kansas	Oklahoma
Michigan	South Dakota
Minnesota	Wisconsin
Missouri	

Western Zone (Zone IV)

Alaska	Montana
American Samoa	Nevada
Arizona	New Mexico
California	Oregon
Colorado	Texas
Guam	Utah
Hawaii	Washington
Idaho	Wyoming

INSURANCE REGULATORY INFORMATION SYSTEM (IRIS)

In response to relatively widespread insurer insolvencies over the past couple of decades, the NAIC has adopted and currently administers the Insurance Regulatory Information System (IRIS), under which insurers submit copies of their annual statements to the NAIC for analysis of certain "test ratios" related to the detection of actual or potential insolvency. The acceptable ranges for the test ratios have not been provided to insurers or made public, but the NAIC does release relevant results concerning particular companies to the concerned regulator-members.

IRIS is divided into two "systems," the first of which is the original IRIS system, consisting of a statistical phase and an analytical phase; the second system is called the Financial Analysis and Solvency Tracking (FAST) system. In 1989, the NAIC Executive Committee decided to release the "statistical phase" of IRIS and the unusual ranges for individual companies, but not the "analytical phase" that results from company examinations and other investigations.[12]

The ratios currently used are shown in Table 6.4. The various items to be compared in the form of ratios are sometimes particular column and line entries (such as "Page 11, Column 2, Line 2c") on the annual statement.

"BEST" RATINGS AND REPORTS

Another important, but "unofficial," solvency safeguard is provided by insurers' financial "Best" ratings. The insurance counterpart to such financial rating services as Moody's and Standard & Poor's is A. M. Best & Co., a company headquartered in New Jersey. The most commonly recognized function of "Best's" is to assign letter ratings, such "A" or "B+," to insurance companies as indicators of their comparative financial strength. In addition to these "overall" ratings, Best's compiles and publishes a large amount of comparative financial information about insurance companies and groups, and about the insurance business in general. Best ratings have no "official" regulatory significance, but they are widely recognized as an important resource for regulators (and others) seeking to monitor the financial condition of insurers. Rating services should, of course, not be confused with rating organizations, which are discussed in Chapter 7.

Table 6.4
NAIC "IRIS" Ratios

PROPERTY-CASUALTY COMPANIES

1.	Gross Premiums to Surplus
1A.	Net Premiums to Surplus
2.	Change in Writings
3.	Surplus Aid to Surplus
4.	Two-Year Overall Operating Ratio
5.	Investment Yield
6.	Change in Surplus
7.	Liabilities to Liquid Assets
8.	Agents' Balances to Surplus
9.	One-Year Reserve Development to Surplus
10.	Two-Year Reserve Development to Surplus
11.	Estimated Current Reserve Deficiency to Surplus

LIFE COMPANIES

1.	Net Change in Capital and Surplus
1a.	Gross Change in Capital and Surplus
2.	Net Gain to Total Income (Including Realized Capital Gains and Losses)
3.	Commissions and Expenses to Premiums and Deposits (Discontinued)
4.	Adequacy of Investment Income
5.	Non-Admitted to Admitted Assets
6.	Total Real Estate and Total Mortgage Loans to Cash and Invested Assets
7.	Total Affiliated Investments to Capital and Surplus
8.	Surplus Relief
9.	Change in Premium
10.	Change in Product Mix
11.	Change in Asset Mix
12.	Change in Reserving Ratio

NOTES

1. See N.Y. Ins. Law Sec. 307(a)(1).
2. See, e.g., N.Y. Ins. Law Sec. 307(b)(1).
3. See, e.g., N.Y. Ins. Law Sec. 309.
4. See, e.g., Ariz. Ins. Code Sec. 20–156.
5. *NAIC Financial Condition Examiners Handbook*, pp. 1–10.
6. *NAIC Market Conduct Examiners Handbook*, pp. V1–V2.
7. See N.Y. Ins. Law Sec. 313(a).
8. *Id*. Sec. 313(b).
9. *Id*. Sec. 310(a)(5) and 311(b).
10. *Id*. Sec. 311(b).
11. *Id*. Sec. 312(b).
12. *NAIC Proceedings 1990*, Vol. 1A, p. 68.

7

Rates and Rating Organizations

RATING LAWS GENERALLY

Insurance rate regulation is a technical and complex subject that relates mostly to property-casualty lines of business, although rates for credit insurance and other kinds of accident and health insurance are also subject to fairly extensive direct controls. The basic purpose of all rate regulation is to prevent the pricing of insurance at levels that are too high, so that insurer's profits are excessive, or too low, so that their solvency is endangered. A secondary purpose of rate regulation is to prohibit inequitable or unfairly discriminatory rates and rate classifications.

The constitutional validity of insurance rate regulation in general, and by the states in particular, has been established in numerous cases, including *German Alliance Ins. Co. v. Kansas*,[1] decided by the United States Supreme Court in 1913. In that case, the Court rejected the insurer's argument that insurance is a "private business" involving only "personal contracts of indemnity." The Court observed in particular that:

the price of insurance is not fixed over the counters of the [insurance] companies by what Adam Smith calls the higgling of the market, but formed in the councils of the underwriters, promulgated in schedules of practically controlling constancy which the applicant for insurance is powerless to oppose and which, therefore, has led to the assertion that the business of insurance is of monopolistic character.[2]

With this scenario in mind, the Court held that the states have the same fundamental power to regulate insurance rates as they have with respect to other matters of public concern, such as transportation and public utility rates.

Life insurance premium rates are usually not regulated in the way that property and casualty rates are, although some states require group life insurance rates to be generally "self-supporting" based upon reasonable mortality and interest assumptions.[3] Premium rates for life insurance are also indirectly regulated by reserving requirements and by: (1) expense limitation provisions, which dictate the maximum sales commissions and other "acquisition" expenses that can be incurred by insurers;[4] (2) surplus accumulation limitations;[5] and (3) surplus apportionment requirements, which mandate the periodic payment of a portion of earned surplus to policyholders in the form of dividends.[6] It is also thought that competition among life insurers, and the ready availability of comparative price information (see Chapter 15), function to keep life insurance premiums from being excessive.

In the area of health insurance, some states place significant controls on the rates for individual health policies through "minimum standards" statutes and regulations which establish minimum loss ratios (i.e., the percentage of premiums paid out as claims), such as 60 or 70 percent,[7] among many other coverage and related criteria for such policies (see Chapter 8). Group health insurance rates, especially those of non-profit health insurers, are also subject to filing and approval requirements in some states.

RATING AND ADVISORY ORGANIZATIONS; RATE FILINGS

Most state insurance laws contain fairly extensive provisions regarding property-casualty rates and rating organizations. (See the columns labeled "Rates/Rating Organizations" in Appendix 3.) Property and casualty rates are usually required not to be "excessive, inadequate, or unfairly discriminatory,"[8] and they are frequently subject to regulatory filing and approval requirements. (The New York statute also prohibits rates which are "destructive of competition or detrimental to the solvency of insurers."[9])

A "rating organization," also called a "rating bureau," has traditionally been an association or similar legal entity formed by insurance companies for the purpose of sharing information and developing rates for use in common.[10] The activities of a now-defunct rating organization, the South-Eastern Underwriters Association, were the basis of the alleged Sherman Act violations that gave rise to the Supreme Court case of *United States v. South-Eastern Underwriters Association* and then to the McCarran-Ferguson Act (see Chapter 1). Those activities included not only the fixing of premium rates, but sometimes also the fixing of commission rates and the making of agreements not to transact reinsurance with non-members. Although current-day rating organizations have more limited purposes, were it not for the antitrust exemptions provided by the McCarran-Ferguson Act, it is almost certain that their activities in setting premium rates would still be considered illegal price-fixing under the Sherman Act.

In current practice, a rating organization is an association or similar non-profit entity authorized by is members, and licensed pursuant to statute,[11] to develop rates, rating plans, underwriting rules, policy forms, and the like, and to file them on behalf of its members with the insurance regulators, where required by law. Such filings, like independent filings by insurers, may be for approval prior to use (a "prior approval" filing), for informational purposes at the time of commencement of use ("file and use") or for informational purposes within a certain time after commencement of use ("use and file"). The lines of business which are likely to involve prior-approval rate filing requirements are workers' compensation, homeowners, private passenger automobile, and medical malpractice insurance, although there is much inconsistency in the various state laws, and even in their apparent purposes. For example, there is no noticeable pattern of regulating commercial insurance rates as opposed to personal insurance rates, or vice versa.

As their name would suggest, informational filings ordinarily do not require an affirmative response from the regulator but, in most cases, informational filings still remain subject to the possibility of affirmative disapproval or orders to discontinue use. Some informational filings, and most prior-approval filings, are subject to statutory "deemer" provisions, which state that a filing will be "deemed approved" by the regulator if it is not affirmatively disapproved within a certain time, such as 30 days, after it is made.

A relatively new variation on prior-approval filing is called "flex rating," currently applicable to certain lines of business in a few states, including New York.[12] Under this system, individual insurers may vary their schedules of rates within a range (usually about 15 to 25 percent) upward or downward from filed and approved base rates. Usually the same schedule of rates must nevertheless be applied to all policies issued at any given point in time.

All policy forms, including endorsements, and sometimes including such related forms as applications for insurance coverage, are normally subject to prior-approval filing requirements in both the property-casualty and the life-health areas. The content of policy forms is often just as important as the corresponding rates, because the forms dictate the breadth or narrowness of coverage and the relative advantages of other terms and conditions.

INSURANCE SERVICES OFFICE (ISO) AND NATIONAL COUNCIL ON COMPENSATION INSURANCE (NCCI); OTHER RATING ORGANIZATIONS

Two major rating organizations—the Insurance Services Office, Inc. (ISO), and the National Council on Compensation Insurance, Inc. (NCCI)—operate on a multi-state or nearly national basis. There are also numerous independent state rating bureaus, some of which are mandated or created by statute, especially for automobile and workers' compensation insurance. For example, the New York Compensation Insurance Rating Board and the Workers' Compensation Rating

Board of California are the rating organizations for workers' compensation insurance in their respective states.

ISO traditionally prepared and filed rates for most property-casualty lines other than workers' compensation. These filings were made on behalf of ISO members, who could then use the rates or develop and file variations on them where required. In recent years, ISO's objectives were changed, and in 1989 it announced plans to phase out its practice of developing full rates, and to produce instead only "advisory loss costs" (that is, "pure" expected claim costs without profit or expense factors). As this system has been phased in line-by-line and state-by-state over the past several years, ISO members have been required to file their own profit and expense factors where required by law.[13]

As of early 1996, NCCI still filed full rates (including profit and expense factors) on behalf of its members in approximately seventeen "administered pricing" states (such as Florida) where it is the authorized rating organization for workers' compensation and employers' liability insurance. In these states, each NCCI member insurer is usually required by law to use these rates for all policies unless it files a "deviation" for approval by the regulator (see the section on deviations, below). If approved, the deviation filing allows the insurer to vary uniformly, upward or downward, from the filed rates by a certain percentage. Member insurers are also unrestricted, as such, in their dividend payment practices on participating policies, although regulatory approval of individual insurers' dividend plans may be required (see Chapter 5).

In approximately 23 other states (such as Georgia and Illinois), which have "competitive rating" laws for workers' compensation insurance, NCCI or the local rating organization files or otherwise disseminates either full advisory rates, which members may adopt if they wish, or advisory "pure premiums" (that is, loss costs without any profit or expense components), to which members must add their own actuarially justified and officially approved profit and expense "loadings."

MANUALS, CLASSIFICATION SYSTEMS, AND RATING PLANS

Rating organizations also commonly compile and publish their rates, rating plans, classifications, and underwriting rules in the form of manuals. These manuals may, in turn, be referred to (directly or indirectly) and incorporated by reference into the premium determination sections of various kinds of insurance policies issued by members of the organization. For example, Section IV(5) of the ISO Commercial General Liability (CGL) policy provides that: "We [the insurance company] will compute all premiums for this Coverage Part in accordance with our rules and rates." In this context, in states whose rating laws apply to general liability insurance, "our" rules and rates means not simply whatever the insurer chooses to apply from time to time, but the rules and rates, usually in the form of a manual, that have been filed by (or on behalf of) the insurer with the respective regulators.

Similarly, Part Five (A) of the NCCI Workers Compensation and Employers Liability policy provides that:

All premiums for this policy will be determined by our manuals of rules, rates, rating plans and classifications. We may change our manuals and apply the changes to this policy if authorized by law or a governmental agency regulating this insurance.

In both of these contexts, underwriting "rules" means uniform rules for the preparation of policies and the rates applicable thereto, not rules that dictate whether or not any particular risk should be insured.

ISO, NCCI, and other rating organizations also prepare and publish recommended or mandatory policy forms and endorsements for use by their members. For example, the NCCI standard Workers Compensation and Employers Liability Policy referred to above is the only generally approved policy form for this line of business in all 44 of the states where private workers compensation insurance is used. Two ISO policy forms that have attracted much attention over the past several years are the claims-made and claims-incurred Commercial General Liability (CGL) policies. Both CGL forms are used, although the claims-made version is much less popular and has not been approved in all states.

An important aspect of NCCI's operations is the administration of a uniform experience rating plan for intrastate and interstate workers' compensation insureds whose annual premiums exceed a certain threshold amount (such as $5,000) which varies by state. Under this plan, an employer's claim experience over a past three-year period is used to calculate an arithmetic "modification factor" (such as 0.75 or 1.25) which is applied to the "manual" premium for a current policy period. The resulting higher or lower premium reflects the probability that the insured's current claim experience will be better or worse than average. The NCCI experience rating plan is set forth in an Experience Rating Plan Manual which is filed and approved in all applicable states, and is then incorporated by reference into each individual policy.

Both NCCI and ISO have also developed and filed standard retrospective rating plans for commercial lines of insurance, including workers' compensation, general liability, and automobile liability. These so-called "retro" plans are similar to self-insurance in that the premium for a current policy period is modified upward or downward after the end of the policy period depending on the insured's claim experience during that period. They are ordinarily used only for large and financially stable insureds who can bear the risk of substantially increased retrospective premium charges. As with the NCCI experience rating plan, these retrospective rating plans are usually set forth in a manual, but their terms are also usually spelled out in a policy endorsement.

DIVIDENDS, DEVIATIONS, AND "CONSENT-TO-RATE" AGREEMENTS

As discussed in Chapter 5, both life-health companies and property-casualty companies may pay dividends to policyholders in certain instances. The payment of dividends on property-casualty policies whose rates are developed by a rating organization is ordinarily a process in which the rating organization is not involved. This is so because, by their nature, policy dividends must be paid with reference to the individual company's experience on a given "book" of business, and not with reference to the overall experience of insurers in the marketplace. Many rating laws provide specifically that a rating organization may not make rules concerning the payment of dividends.[14]

"Deviations" from filed and approved manual rates are authorized by many rating laws.[15] In some states, and for some lines of business, a deviation must consist of a uniform percentage by which the rates for all classifications in a given line of insurance are to be increased or decreased for all insureds. For example, Company X may file and receive approval for a 10 percent downward deviation for all workers' compensation policies it writes, or a 5 percent upward deviation for all of its automobile policies. (Since deviation filings apply to all policies written by a given insurer, insurers with different deviation filings in effect may, within a single holding company's "group," be prepared to offer a range of rates for different insureds, depending on the degree of risk involved and other relevant factors.) In other states, and for other lines of business, a deviation may consist of non-uniform departures from manual rates, or even a completely different rating structure.

Most casualty rating laws also allow for the use, on a case-by-case basis, of rates higher than the filed and approved rates if the insured consents in writing to the use of the higher rate.[16] These "consent-to-rate" agreements must ordinarily be filed with the regulator, sometimes for prior approval, together with an explanation of the "reasons therefor."[17] In New York, under what is commonly called the "Free Trade Zone" legislation, specially licensed insurers called "special risk insurers" are exempt from rate and form filing requirements with respect to certain large or unusual risks.[18]

STATISTICAL REPORTING AND DATA COLLECTION

Rating organizations develop and file rates and other components of rating systems based largely on historical data furnished to them by their members and other insurers. Based on the "law of large numbers," which posits that larger quantities of statistics provide more meaningful or "credible" predictive results, insurance rate-making bodies endeavor to collect premium, loss, and expense data from the largest possible "statistical base."

In many states, reporting of data for a designated bureau or agency is required by statute for certain lines of business,[19] and some reporting is usually an obligation of membership in a rating organization as well. In the field of workers' compensation and employers' liability insurance, the Unit Statistical Plan administered by the National Council on Compensation Insurance is central to the preparation of overall rate level revisions and to the promulgation of individual risk experience ratings. ISO also engages in extensive collection of premium and loss data from its members for the purpose of developing historical "loss costs."

"UNISEX" RATING

So-called "unisex" rating is becoming increasingly popular, despite the fact that, for example, on the whole, women live longer than men and male drivers have more automobile accidents than female drivers. These statistical patterns have traditionally been reflected in the rates insurers charge for life insurance, annuities, automobile insurance, and perhaps some other coverages.

The question whether insurance rates should be based on the sex of the person insured, even when one sex or the other generally presents a greater insurance risk, is a subject of ongoing controversy in the courts and legislatures. For example, in 1978 the United States Supreme Court held in *Manhart v. City of Los Angeles Department of Water and Power*[20] that unequal contribution rates for male and female participants in a public employees' pension plan violated Title VII of the Civil Rights Act of 1964. In a later case, *Arizona Governing Committee for Tax Deferred Annuity and Deferred Compensation Plans v. Norris*,[21] also based on the Civil Rights Act, the Court held that an employer could not legally offer female employees any retirement options which provided lower monthly benefits than those afforded to similarly situated male employees.

In a similar vein, state courts have sometimes held that sex-based insurance rates, such as those for automobile insurance, violate the state's statutes, constitution, or public policy. For example, in 1982 the Pennsylvania insurance commissioner disapproved sex-based automobile insurance rates on the basis of the state constitution's Equal Rights Amendment, and the commissioner's decision was upheld in state court proceedings.[22] Following an amendment to the rating law which expressly permitted the use of sex as a rating factor, an action was brought to enjoin enforcement of the new rating law provision. A Commonwealth court held that the statute violated the Equal Rights Amendment and was therefore unconstitutional.[23]

In a few states, such as Massachusetts[24] and Michigan,[25] "unisex" rates for males and females are now required by statute for certain kinds of insurance. In Montana, the use of sex-based rates for any form of insurance has been prohibited since 1986.[26]

NOTES

1. 233 U.S. 389 (1913).
2. *Id.* at 416.

3. See N.Y. Ins. Dept. Regulations Part 155, Sec. 155.1.

4. See N.Y. Ins. Law Sec. 4228.

5. *Id.* Sec. 4219.

6. *Id.* Sec. 4231.

7. *Id.* Sec. 3217.

8. *Id.* Sec. 2303.

9. *Id.*

10. See N.Y. Ins. Law Sec. 2313(a).

11. *Id.*

12. N.Y. Ins. Law Sec. 2344.

13. See Krohm, "Implications of ISO's Change to Loss Cost Filing for Rate Regulation," 8 *Journal of Insurance Regulation* 316 (March 1990).

14. See N.Y. Ins. Law Sec. 2313(m).

15. See, e.g., N.Y. Ins. Law Sec. 2339.

16. *Id.* Sec. 2309.

17. *Id.*

18. N.Y. Ins. Law Sec. 6301 and N.Y. Ins. Dept. Regulation 86.

19. See, e.g., N.Y. Ins. Law Sec. 2325.

20. 435 U.S. 702 (1978).

21. 463 U.S. 1073 (1983).

22. *Hartford Acc. & Indem. Co. v. Ins. Commissioner*, 442 A.2d 382 (Pa. 1982).

23. *Bartholomew v. Foster*, 541 A.2d 393 (Pa. Commonwlth. 1988), aff'd 563 A.2d 1390 (Pa. 1989).

24. Mass. Ins. Code Sec. 175E:4(d) (motor vehicle insurance).

25. Mich. Ins. Code Sec. 500.2111(5) (automobile insurance).

26. Mont. Ins. Code Sec. 49–2–309.

8

Insurance Contracts

The tangible evidence of the "product" sold by any insurance company is, of course, the insurance policy or contract. Traditionally these policies and contracts have been technical legal documents, standardized on the part of the insurer or even uniformly among insurers, and not subject to much, if any, negotiation with insureds. An important subject of insurance regulation, therefore, is the content and format of insurance contracts, and the promotion of fairness in their terms and conditions.

All personal insurance contracts can be classified as either "individual" or "group," the latter kind being common only in the field of life insurance, health insurance, and annuities. As the names suggest, individual contracts usually involve direct obligations between the insurer and person insured (in the sense of the person having an "insurable interest," as discussed below). By contrast, the direct parties to a group contract are usually an insurer and an employer, labor organization, or other membership association acting not for itself but on behalf of its employees or members (who in turn have an insurable interest). Each person insured under a group contract nevertheless receives a "certificate" or some other written evidence of coverage in most instances.

Commercial policies can be classified as either "monoline" or "package" (also called "multi-peril") depending upon whether they provide only one kind of property or liability coverage, or a combination thereof. For example, a personal auto policy is a monoline policy, but a combination of commercial property, auto, and general liability under one integrated contract is a package or multi-peril policy.

SIMPLIFICATION AND "READABILITY"

During the 1970's, as consumer protection became a popular concern, various states began to require the linguistic simplification of certain kinds of insurance policies, either by statute or regulation. The kinds of policies involved were generally those sold directly to consumers, such as life, automobile, and homeowners' policies, but most commercial policies gradually came to be "simplified" as well, whether or not required by law.

The basic principle of insurance policy simplification is that policies should be "readable" and written in "plain English," without unnecessary legal or other technical terminology, and in relatively simple forms of grammar and syntax. Readability of insurance contracts for regulatory purposes is usually judged by reference to the "Flesch Reading Ease Test,"[1] under which any given text is rated numerically based upon the average number of syllables per word and the average number of words per sentence. Sentences that are separated into parts by colons or semicolons are usually treated as separate sentences, so that the Flesch score is improved by the use of such punctuation. There may also be type size requirements, such as a minimum "ten-point" size (approximately $10/72$ of an inch) for the main portion of any text.

CONFORMITY TO STATUTE; REPRESENTATIONS AND WARRANTIES

Because the variety of insurance policy forms (including riders, endorsements, and schedules) is virtually unlimited, and because thorough regulatory scrutiny of all forms prior to their use is not always possible, most state insurance laws include a provision which states that any policy issued in violation of the insurance laws is automatically deemed to be amended to conform to the applicable requirements.[2] This concept is frequently written into the policy itself in a "conformity to statute" or similar provision through which the policy automatically corrects or completes itself as to any overlooked or otherwise omitted regulatory requirements.

Another very common kind of statutory provision, essential to creating a valid and enforceable insurance contract between the parties, concerns the representations made by the insured to the insurer prior to, or at the time of, policy issuance. State insurance laws usually provide that, at least with respect to life and health insurance, any statements (such as statements about a person's health) made by or on behalf of the insured or other applicant as part of the application for insurance, or otherwise to induce the issuance of a policy, are deemed to be "representations" and not "warranties."[3]

Whereas a breach of warranty in itself can make an insurance contract voidable (i.e., invalid at the insurer's option), a representation must be false and "material" in order to produce the same effect. A representation generally is not material to the making of an insurance contract unless the insurer would have refused to make the contract if it had known the representation was false. These kinds of statutory provisions therefore protect the insured from inadvertently making a warranty which could invalidate the policy. They also condone insureds' misrepresentations which are not essential to insurers' underwriting decisions. Closely related to these provisions regarding misrepresentation are the required incontestability provisions for life and health insurance discussed below.

LIFE AND HEALTH INSURANCE: INCONTESTABILITY AND OTHER REQUIRED PROVISIONS

Life and health insurance policy forms, including group policies and certificates of coverage, riders, endorsements, and applications, usually must be filed with the regulator and approved before use.[4] The variety of the required, prohibited, and permissible provisions in the various jurisdictions is enormous, most notably in the area of mandated health insurance coverages, where as many as 800-odd different requirements can be counted.[5] The most common and most important general requirements include the following.

1. Individual life policies must provide for: a 31-day grace period for payment of premiums;[6] incontestability (i.e., no contesting of contractual validity based on misrepresentation) after two years from policy issuance;[7] attachment of a copy of the insured's application as part of the "entire contract";[8] "nonforfeiture values" including a guaranteed cash surrender value and policy loan value when applicable to the plan of insurance involved (i.e., whole life versus term insurance);[9] and the insured's option of reinstatement (subject to evidence of insurability) within two or three years after a lapse due to nonpayment of premiums.[10] (Nonforfeiture values are practically dictated by the nature of "level premium" and similar whole life policies, as to which the premiums paid in earlier years, when the risk of death is small, are much more than is needed to pay the cost of insurance protection.)

2. Individual accident and health policies are sometimes required to contain strictly standardized provisions regarding such matters as the "entire contract;" incontestability after two or three years; notice, proof, and payment of claims; physical examinations of the insured after a claim is made; other applicable insurance policies; and cancellation or non-renewal (when applicable).[11]

3. Group life policy standard provisions may relate to: eligibility for coverage based on membership in the group; incontestability; issuance of individual certificates of insurance to insured group members; payment of life insurance proceeds to the insured's estate as an ultimate beneficiary if the named beneficiaries are already deceased; and rights of conversion to individual coverage upon termination of the group policy.[12]

4. Group accident and health policies may be required to provide for: eligibility of new group members; issuance of individual certificates; notice, proof, and payment of claims; physical examinations of the insured; and group members' rights to convert to individual coverage.[13]

INSURABLE INTEREST: LIFE INSURANCE

The doctrine of insurable interest is basically a common-law creation,[14] but it is now frequently embodied in statutes, sometimes in an elaborated form. Most state laws expressly require the applicant for life insurance to have an insurable interest in the proposed insured (if the insured is someone other than the applicant, such as a spouse or parent).[15] Insurable interest in human life may be defined as either a "substantial interest engendered by love and affection" or a "lawful and substantial economic interest in the continued life, health, or bodily safety of the person insured."[16] Some states also have statutory versions of the judicially recognized rule that the consent of the person insured is required, regardless of insurable interest, in order for any life insurance contract to be valid and enforceable.[17]

New York is virtually unique in having extremely detailed requirements as to the amounts of insurance that can lawfully be issued on the lives of minor children.[18] Many states, including New York, also have statutes that permit minors over the age of 14 or 15 years to purchase and own life insurance policies on their own lives or on the lives of others, despite the fact that they are too young to enter into binding contracts generally.[19]

INSURABLE INTEREST: PROPERTY AND CASUALTY INSURANCE

Insurable interest historically has also been a common-law requirement in the area of property insurance. In addition, some states have statutory provisions that define and require an insurable interest in property, in terms such as: "any lawful and substantial economic interest in the safety or preservation of property from loss, destruction or pecuniary damage."[20] The question whether an insurable interest must exist at the time of an insured loss, or only at the time of policy issuance, is sometimes presented under such laws. In such cases, it is usually held that the interest must exist at the time of the loss.[21]

PROPERTY-CASUALTY POLICY FORMS

Policy forms, including applications and endorsements, for property and casualty insurance are frequently subject to filing and approval requirements. A standard fire insurance policy is required by statute in some states including New York,[22] with some variations from state to state. The standard fire policy provides, among other things, that: the measure of loss will be the "actual cash value of the property at the time of loss," not to exceed the replacement cost, and without allowance for business interruption losses; property such as currency and securities is not insured; perils such as war and revolution are not covered; the amount of any insured loss will be arbitrated if the insurer and insured cannot agree about it; and losses are payable 60 days after the amount is agreed upon.

The policy forms developed and filed by the Insurance Services Office, Inc. (for lines other than workers' compensation and employers' liability) and the National Council on Compensation Insurance, Inc. (for workers' compensation and employers' liability) are widely used as "standard" or "advisory" by their insurer members (see Chapter 7). The most important of the ISO forms are the personal auto, homeowners, commercial auto, commercial property, and commercial general liability coverage forms.

CANCELLATION AND NON-RENEWAL OF POLICIES

A relatively recent phenomenon is the large number of state laws that place restrictions on the timing of, and acceptable reasons for, cancellation and non-renewal of various kinds of property-casualty policies. These policies were traditionally cancellable at the insurer's discretion on relatively short notice, such as ten days. Many laws now require longer notice periods, such as 30 days or more, and limit the permissible reasons for cancellation to such things as non-payment of premium, discovery of fraud or misrepresentation, violation of safety rules, or other specific increased hazards.[23] Non-renewal of policies may require considerable advance notice, such as 60 days before expiration.[24] If an insurer's exact compliance with a cancellation or non-renewal requirement is questionable, the insured may have coverage beyond the expiration date or may be entitled to damages for the increased cost of replacement coverage.

AUTOMOBILE "FINANCIAL RESPONSIBILITY" AND "NO-FAULT" LAWS; UNINSURED MOTORIST FUNDS

Automobile liability insurance is required of vehicle owners in all or nearly all states and the District of Columbia,[25] either under a "financial responsibility" law (which requires evidence of financial responsibility after an accident, as a condition to continuing one's registration) or a compulsory insurance law (which requires proof of insurance at the time of registration and thereafter). These laws are intended to prevent drivers without adequate financial resources from operating automobiles. Many of them require minimum limits of liability insurance in the range of $10,000 to $25,000 per injured person, per accident, and $20,000 to $50,000 in the aggregate per accident.[26] In New York, the required limits as of 1996 are: $25,000 for injury to one person and $50,000 for injury to more than one person in any one accident; $50,000 for the death of any one person and $100,000 for the death of more than one person in any one accident; and $10,000 for property damage in any one accident.[27]

Assigned risk plans (see Chapter 9) of one kind or another are in place in all states except Maryland (where a state insurance fund is used instead) to provide coverage through licensed insurers to most drivers whose driving records or other risk characteristics disqualify them for voluntary coverage directly from a licensed insurer. Most of these plans are organized under a statute that makes participation by all licensed insurers mandatory.[28]

Since the early 1970's, beginning with Massachusetts in 1971, 28 states[29] have enacted versions of "no-fault" automobile insurance laws (sometimes called automobile "reparations" acts) which require, or give the insured an option to purchase, coverage under which injured persons are entitled to recover limited medical and income replacement benefits from their own insurers. This "first-party" insurance is payable regardless of who was at fault in causing the accident, or even if there was no fault on anyone's part. Suits for damages on account of personal injuries are frequently restricted to cases involving "serious injury," as defined in the applicable law, or death. When the definition of "serious injury" is related to a dollar amount of medical and other expenses, it is usually called a "monetary threshold." When it is a verbal, medical description of certain kinds of injuries, it is called a "verbal threshold."

In New York, the basic provisions of the no-fault law, called the "Comprehensive Motor Vehicle Reparations Act,"[30] are as follows.

1. "Basic economic loss" is defined as medical expenses, loss of earnings up to $2,000 per month within three years after the accident, and other expenses up to $25 per day; all of the foregoing are subject to a combined limit of $50,000.

2. "Non-economic loss" is defined as pain and suffering and other non-monetary detriment.

3. "Serious injury" is defined as death, dismemberment or disfigurement, a fracture, permanent loss of use of a bodily organ or member, significant limitation of use of a bodily function or system, or a non-permanent injury which disables an injured person for at least 90 days (a "verbal threshold").

4. Every automobile liability policy must provide first-party benefits to all injured persons, other than occupants of another vehicle, for "basic economic loss" resulting from a New York accident.

5. There is no right of recovery on the part of one "covered person" against another "covered person" by way of a negligence action for "non-economic loss," except in case of a "serious injury," or in any case for "basic economic loss." (A "covered person" is a pedestrian; an owner, operator, or occupant of an insured vehicle; or another person entitled to no-fault benefits, as set forth in the statute.)

A few states, including New York,[31] also have statutes that establish a fund to which licensed insurers must contribute, for the purpose of paying claims against uninsured, underinsured, or unidentified ("hit-and-run") motorists. The New York fund, called the Motor Vehicle Accident Indemnification Corporation, will pay up to the New York minimum limits of liability insurance discussed above, less any insurance or assets of the "financially irresponsible motorist" which are recoverable.[32] In other states, uninsured motorist coverage (under which the injured person's own insurer pays on the basis of the uninsured motorist's fault) may be mandatory, or insurers may be required to offer it as an option.

NOTES

1. See N.Y. Ins. Law Sec. 3102(c).
2. *Id.* Sec. 3103.
3. *Id.* Sec. 3204(c).
4. *Id.* Sec. 3201(b).
5. Nielson et al., "The Efficacy of Mandated Coverage for AIDS," 7 *Journal of Insurance Regulation* 440 (June 1989).
6. See N.Y. Ins. Law Sec. 3203(a)(1).
7. *Id.* Sec. 3203(a)(3).
8. *Id.* Sec. 3203(a)(4).
9. *Id.* Sec. 3203(a)(7) and (8).
10. *Id.* Sec. 3202(a)(10).
11. *Id.* Sec. 3216.
12. *Id.* Sec. 3220.
13. *Id.* Sec. 3221.
14. Meyer, *Life and Health Insurance Law* (Rochester, N.Y.: Lawyers Co-operative Pub. Co., 1972, 1995), Sec. 4:1.
15. See N.Y. Ins. Law Sec. 3205.
16. *Id.*
17. Meyer, *op. cit.*, Sec. 4:6; N.Y. Ins. Law Sec. 3205(c).
18. Meyer, *Id.*; N.Y. Ins. Law Sec. 3207.
19. See N.Y. Ins. Law Sec. 3207; N.J.S.A. 17B:24–2; Ill. Ins. Law Sec. 242.
20. See N.Y. Ins. Law Sec. 3401.
21. *Id.* Sec. 3404.
22. *Id.* Sec. 3425–3426.
23. *Id.* Sec. 3429; Ill. Ins. Law Sec. 155.22.
24. See, e.g., N.Y. Ins. Law Sec. 3429.
25. *1997 Property-Casualty Fact Book* (New York: Insurance Information Institute, 1997), pp. 114–115.
26. *Id.* p. 104.
27. N.Y. Vehicle & Traffic Law Sec. 311(4).
28. See N.Y. Ins. Law Sec. 5301–5304.
29. *Supra* Note 25 at pp. 116–117.
30. N.Y. Ins. Law Sec. 5101–5108.
31. *Id.* Sec. 5201–5225.
32. *Id.* Sec. 5210.

9

Assigned Risk Plans and Other Residual Market Mechanisms

ASSIGNED RISK PLANS GENERALLY

It is self-evident that, in general, insurance contracts are voluntarily entered into by insurers and insureds. There are, however, various kinds of "compulsory" insurance under state and federal laws, including automobile liability and workers' compensation insurance. Also, certain kinds of insurance are practical necessities for some people, such as medical malpractice insurance for physicians.

The usual, "voluntary" market of insurers may not always accommodate the demand for these essential coverages, for various reasons, including: (1) the inadequacy (i.e., excessively low level) of rates in some states or lines of business where rates are governmentally controlled (see Chapter 7); (2) the poor or unpredictable underwriting results for certain coverages, such as medical malpractice or liquor liability; and (3) the undesirability of certain individual risks, such as drivers with poor driving records or employers with bad safety records. Most insurance laws, therefore, either authorize or require insurers to participate in plans or "mechanisms" to provide collectively the coverages that they are unwilling to provide independently. Whether such plans are voluntary on the part of insurers or not, the coverages provided under them are commonly referred to as being in the "involuntary market," or the "residual market." Yet another term for approximately the same thing is "assigned risk."

Although some statutes and regulations governing residual market mechanisms are very specific and detailed, many states have enacted (instead or in addition) very general laws that permit insurers to enter into "risk sharing plans" or "risk apportionment agreements," usually in language similar to the following:

Agreements may be made among insurers with respect to the equitable apportionment among them of insurance which may be afforded applicants who are in good faith entitled to but unable to procure such insurance through ordinary methods, and such insurers may agree among themselves upon the use of reasonable rate modifications subject to the approval of the commissioner.[1]

Laws of this kind provide a degree of state regulation over such plans or agreements, and at the same time exempt them (to the extent of that regulation) from the application of the federal antitrust laws, by virtue of the McCarran-Ferguson Act (see Chapter 1).

The usual characteristics of a residual market mechanism are (1) required participation by all licensed insurers, either as direct insurers, as reinsurers, or through assessments; and (2) nearly universal eligibility among potential insureds. The grounds for disqualification of an applicant are usually limited to a demonstrated lack of "good faith" by reason of nonpayment of premiums, abandonment of insured buildings, willful disregard of reasonable safety requirements, or similar conduct. The amounts of insurance available are often less than what might be available in the voluntary marketplace, and the premiums are sometimes higher for comparable amounts of coverage. There may also be premium surcharges based upon claim histories or other factors.

AUTOMOBILE PLANS AND JOINT UNDERWRITING ASSOCIATIONS (JUAs)

As discussed in Chapter 8, most states and the District of Columbia have laws that make the purchase of automobile liability insurance compulsory.[2] In order to guarantee the availability of automobile insurance, personal automobile residual market or assigned risk plans exist in all 50 states and the District of Columbia.[3] Most of the jurisdictions also have commercial automobile residual market mechanisms. The plans normally provide at least the minimum limits of liability coverage required by state law, plus no-fault coverage, where required (see Chapter 8), and certain amounts of first-party physical damage ("collision" and "comprehensive") coverage. The plans fall into four general categories, as follows:

1. a "pure" assigned risk plan under which each licensed insured receives direct assignments of applicants at random and directly insures each assigned applicant for the insurer's own account (i.e., without reinsurance, other than independently obtained reinsurance, if available);

2. a "joint underwriting association" which places applicants with a limited number of volunteer "servicing carriers" who then issue policies that are partly or entirely reinsured by the members of the association (so that the losses are shared by all members in proportion to their voluntary market share, or a similar standard of measurement);

3. a reinsurance facility, which is a combination of categories 1 and 2, whereby each member receives assignments and automatically obtains reinsurance from a facility or association composed of all members; and

4. a state-sponsored insurance fund (in Maryland only), which is organized and operated separately from any private insurer but subsidized to some extent by assessments from all licensed automobile insurers.[4]

Residual market plans for other lines of insurance commonly fall into one or the other of these categories as well.

Automobile plans of one variety or another covered approximately 5.9 million insured automobiles in 1994, with the highest numbers occurring in New York (1.3 million), North Carolina (1.2 million), and South Carolina (0.9 million).[5] The Automobile Insurance Plans Service Office (AIPSO) is an insurer-sponsored association which collects statistics and develops rates and procedures for these plans.[6]

WORKERS' COMPENSATION PLANS AND POOLS

Workers' compensation laws were enacted in all states and the District of Columbia between 1914 and 1949. These laws impose a limited no-fault liability on employers for job-related injuries and illnesses of their employees, and they generally require that liability to be insured or self-insured under stringent controls. Since self-insurance is usually possible only for very large and well-capitalized businesses, most employers in the United States must obtain workers' compensation insurance from some source.

Six states (Nevada, North Dakota, Ohio, Washington, West Virginia, and Wyoming) have state-sponsored insurance funds that are called "monopolistic" or "exclusive" state funds, meaning that they are the required source, and the only source of coverage permitted, within the respective states. Twenty-two other states[7] have state insurance funds that are competitive with private insurers, and most of these funds will accept almost any applicant, without regard to insurability. Such funds are sometimes referred to as "insurers of last resort," and there is usually no need for an assigned risk plan in states that have them.

In most other states, residual market plans, basically similar to the joint underwriting associations described above, operate to provide insurance for employers who cannot obtain it otherwise. A unique feature of these plans is their common management by the National Council on Compensation Insurance (NCCI), a multi-state statistical and rating organization (see Chapter 7) which has over 700 insurer members. In recent years, these plans have accounted for as much as 20 percent or more of the total private workers' compensation market, measured by written premiums.

Each policy issued by one of several volunteer servicing carriers under an NCCI-administered plan is completely reinsured by the members of the National Workers Compensation Reinsurance Pool (NWCRP), except for policies covering employers in the states of Maine, Massachusetts, and New Mexico, which have separate plans and reinsurance pools mandated by state law.[8] The NWCRP membership includes almost all insurers writing workers' compensation insurance in each covered state. The members afford the servicing carriers reinsurance for 100% of losses, in proportion to the members' written premiums by state on a policy-year and calendar-year basis. Basically, losses arising out of a given policy year (i.e., all policies issued or renewed during that year) are paid by the servicing carriers and reimbursed to them by the members in proportion to the members' calendar-year written premiums corresponding to that policy year. The servicing carriers are typically allowed to retain approximately 30 percent of the premium as a "servicing allowance" to cover underwriting, loss adjustment, inspection, and other expenses.

FIRE INSURANCE (FAIR) PLANS

Although it is not required by law, fire and other hazard insurance on privately owned houses and buildings is invariably required by banks and other lenders in connection with mortgage financing, and is normally dictated by prudence in any event. To facilitate the acquisition and ownership of such properties in depressed urban neighborhoods and other geographical areas that are not usually considered to be desirable insurance risks, some state laws create associations or plans (usually called FAIR plans, an acronym for "Fair Access to Insurance Requirements") which require participation by all licensed insurers who write fire insurance. Qualified FAIR plans are entitled to federal reinsurance, under the National Insurance Development Program, with regard to losses from riots and other civil disorders.[9]

FAIR plans currently exist in 31 states and the District of Columbia.[10] In New York, the plan takes the form of an association called the New York Property Insurance Underwriting Association (NYPIUA),[11] which is authorized to function much like an insurance company in issuing policies, collecting premiums, and paying claims. Its deficits are subsidized by all insurers licensed to write and writing fire insurance in New York State.[12]

Typical features of a FAIR plan include the following.

1. The operations of the plan are governed by a Board of Directors or similar body, elected by the insurer members of the plan at annual membership meetings.

2. Day-to-day operations are handled by officers elected by the Board, and in some cases by other employees of the plan.

3. The plan rules specify what properties are ineligible for coverage, such as: unoccupied or abandoned buildings; buildings on which real property taxes are seriously delinquent; buildings with serious uncorrected safety violations; buildings in danger of collapse or under a demolition order; buildings which have been subject to numerous fire losses within a certain time period; and buildings owned by persons who have been convicted of arson or insurance fraud.

4. The plan rules govern the maximum amounts of coverage available for buildings of different kinds of construction (such as frame, masonry, and fire-resistive construction) and which serve different purposes (such as apartment buildings, commercial buildings, and schools).

5. The plan rules govern the "binding" (i.e., the automatic effectiveness) of coverage at a specified time, such as a few days, after a properly completed application is received by the plan, and the applicable rates, such as ISO-based rates (see Chapter 7).

6. The plan rules contain the premium payment requirements, such as the minimum deposit premium payable and the terms of subsequent installment payments, if any, and prescribe the amount of commission (such as 10 percent) payable to the producer chosen by the insured to place the coverage.[13]

The FAIR Plans issued or renewed approximately 952,000 policies in 1995.[14]

MISCELLANEOUS PLANS

Residual market plans of one variety or another also exist in some states for lines of business such as medical malpractice, municipal liability, liquor liability, and individual health insurance.[15] Various Blue Cross and Blue Shield organizations also offer health insurance during "open enrollment" periods to individuals regardless of their health history or present condition.

Market Assistance Plans (MAPs) are utilized in some states to provide commercial applicants with a means of automatic referral, usually under the auspices of the insurance department, to one or more insurers who may be willing to provide coverage voluntarily.

NOTES

1. Iowa Insurance Code Sec. 515A.15.
2. *1997 Property-Casualty Fact Book* (New York: Insurance Information Institute, 1997), pp. 114–115.
3. *Id.* p. 42.
4. Maryland Ins. Code Sec. 243 et seq.
5. *Supra* Note 2 at p. 43.
6. *Id.* p. 130.
7. *Survey of Workers' Compensation Laws* (Schaumburg, Ill.: Alliance of American Insurers, 1995), pp. 57–58.
8. Maine Ins. Code Sec. 2366 et seq.; Mass. Statutes Sec. 152:65C; N. Mex. Ins. Code Sec. 59A–33–1 et seq.
9. 12 U.S.C. Sec. 1749 bbb et seq.
10. *Supra* Note 2 at p. 44.
11. N.Y. Ins. Law Sec. 5401 et seq.
12. *Id.* Sec. 5405.

    13. New York Property Insurance Underwriting Association, Plan of Operation.
    14. *Supra* Note 2 at p. 44.
    15. See, e.g., N.Y. Ins. Law Sec. 5001 et seq. (Medical Malpractice Insurance Association).

10

Agents, Brokers, and Other Representatives

AGENTS, BROKERS, AND "PRODUCERS"

Insurance policies are sold by insurers through direct marketing methods, such as branch offices or the mail, and through independent representatives, usually called "agents" or "brokers." These representatives not only procure customers and arrange for the issuance and renewal of policies, but they also usually act as servicing representatives with regard to claims, premium payments and refunds, and various kinds of policy changes.

Life insurance is more often marketed and serviced by "full-time" agents who represent only one insurer or group of insurers, and who may even be considered employees of the insurer for tax and other purposes. Property-casualty insurance, on the other hand, usually involves "independent agents" or brokers who represent or deal with various different insurers. This latter scenario is commonly referred to as the "American Agency System," which may be more completely described as follows:

Independent agents usually represent several insurance companies and try to insure the risk according to availability of coverage and the most favorable price. Independent agents are paid a commission in the form of a percentage of the premiums generated by the policy sold. They own all the records of the policies sold and have the right to solicit renewals. They are not restricted to maintaining business with just one company and can transfer the business upon renewal to another company.[1]

An important component of this description is the concept of "renewals," also referred to as "expirations." The agent's contractual right to divert existing business away from an insurer he or she currently represents gives the agent a remarkable degree of financial and legal independence. Sometimes it is even said that an agent or broker owns his or her "book of business." The status of "independent insurance agent" is expressly recognized in New York, which prohibits the use of that term in advertising or otherwise by anyone who does not possess the requisite characteristics.[2]

By convention, property-casualty insurers are sometimes divided into categories based on their primary marketing method. A "direct writer" is an insurer, commonly a mutual company, that sells policies through representatives who are employees of the company and are compensated at least partially by a salary. An "agency" or "brokerage" company is an insurer that sells primarily through independent contractors who are legal representatives of the company for many purposes, but are free to deal with one, several, or many different insurers.

Both agents and brokers are usually compensated solely or primarily by commissions, that is, by payments contingent upon production of business and proportional to the amount of premiums produced. Compensation to such persons may also include "profit-sharing" (additional commissions contingent on the profitability of the business produced) and "servicing fees" which represent payment for providing advice and services to insureds apart from the initial sale transaction.

LICENSING REQUIREMENTS GENERALLY

Virtually all state insurance codes implicitly recognize that the financial and legal independence of many sales representatives from the insurers they represent requires certain safeguards for the benefit of the insurers and the buying public alike. First of all, every state has some form of licensing requirement for agents, brokers, and similar representatives. (See the columns labeled "Agent/ Broker Licensing" in Appendix 3.) Normally, different licenses are required for life-health business and for property-casualty business (although some states, like New York, do not provide for agents and brokers in both categories).[3] Applicants often must meet certain educational criteria, such as completion of a prescribed training course given by an approved institution, and invariably must pass a written test or series of tests.[4] Both the training course and the test or tests may be waived in some states if the applicant has earned the Chartered Life Underwriter (C.L.U.) or Chartered Property and Casualty Underwriter (C.P.C.U.) designation.[5]

The activities that constitute acting as an agent or broker are usually defined quite precisely in the licensing statutes. For example, the New York statute defines an "insurance agent" as "any authorized or acknowledged agent of an insurer . . . and any sub-agent or representative of such an agent, who act as such in the solicitation of, negotiation for, or procurement or making of, an insurance or annuity contract. . . ."[6] It also excludes from the category of agent any regular, salaried employee or officer of an insurer who does not solicit or accept orders from the public outside of the insurer's office, and does not receive any commissions or other compensation contingent upon the amount of business done.[7] Under such a provision, an employee who receives commissions is nevertheless considered an agent and therefore must be licensed. The New York definition of "insurance broker" is similar, except that a broker is one who acts "on behalf of an insured other than himself,"[8] and the corresponding exclusion relates to regular, salaried employees of an insured who act with regard to coverages for the insured.[9]

Secondly, the licensing statutes of most states reflect the different kinds of sales representation occurring in the marketplace, so that the requirements for being licensed as an agent typically differ from those applicable to a broker. In some states, in addition to whatever agency agreements insurers and agents may voluntarily enter into, agents must be administratively "appointed" by the insurer or insurers they intend to represent. The appointment takes the form of a written statement filed by each appointing insurer with the insurance regulator.[10] Revocation of the appointment by another filing with the regulator normally terminates the agency status for regulatory purposes.[11] Normally, no particular form of appointment or agreement is required before a broker places business with an insurer, although at least an oral agreement regarding commission rates and accounting procedures is customary.

A small number of states, including Texas[12] and Michigan,[13] do not recognize the status of a broker at all, so that every insurance representative is appointed by, and licensed as, an agent of one or more insurers. At least two states, New Jersey[14] and Illinois,[15] use the neutral term "producer" to describe all business-producing insurance representatives.

The key provision of an agents' or brokers' licensing statute normally states that no person shall act as an agent or broker (as defined in the statute), hold himself or herself out to members of the public as such, or receive any money, fee, or commission as such, without being duly licensed.[16] A complementary provision usually prohibits insurers from paying any compensation to unlicensed persons who act as agents or brokers.[17] Exceptions are frequently provided for licensed attorneys, actuaries, and certified public accountants who provide professional services in connection with insurance transactions.[18]

RESTRICTIONS ON "CONTROLLED BUSINESS"

Payment of commissions to an agent or agency closely related to a given insured may be a way to circumvent the anti-rebating laws (see the section on commissions and rebating, below). For example, an industrial corporation could profit by creating its own "captive" agency to procure all of its coverages, thereby indirectly receiving discounts in the form of commissions on its own business. Primarily for this reason, insurance producers are commonly prohibited from profiting on the placement of substantial amounts of business on behalf of affiliates, that is, persons or entities who control them, by whom they are controlled, or who are under common control with them. For example, New York prohibits an agent or broker from retaining commissions on such "controlled business'' which exceeds 5 percent of the agent's or broker's total annual commissions.[19]

CORPORATE AND NON-RESIDENT LICENSES

In most states, insurance agents and brokers may be either natural persons or business entities, such as corporations or partnerships. One notable exception is Florida, where only natural persons may be licensed as agents.[20] Normally every natural person acting as an agent within the organization of a corporate or partnership agency must also be licensed individually. For example, in the case of the New York statute quoted above, any "sub-agent or other representative" of an agent, who acts as such in insurance transactions, is considered an agent as well, and therefore must be licensed.

Many states also have special licensing provisions for "non-resident" agents and brokers, usually defined as individuals who (1) do not reside in the state in question, and (2) do not have an office in that state, but (3) are licensed as agents or brokers in another state where they maintain an office.[21] A significant requirement affecting non-resident agents and brokers is that relating to the "countersignature" of a resident agent or broker which, under many state laws, must be affixed to each policy negotiated by the non-resident.[22]

DURATION, REVOCATION, AND SUSPENSION OF LICENSES

Agents' and brokers' licenses ordinarily expire after a certain period, such as one year or two years, and they must be renewed by submission of a renewal application, payment of a renewal fee, or both. In New York, agents' licenses had an indefinite duration until 1985, when the statute was amended to provide for two-year terms expiring uniformly on June 30 of odd-numbered years.[23]

Under most licensing statutes, licenses may be revoked by the regulator for such predictable reasons as fraud, dishonesty, incompetence, untrustworthiness, or certain specific violations of the insurance laws.[24] Revocation of a person's or entity's license may disqualify the former licensee from being employed by, or in any way affiliated with, another licensee in the future, except perhaps in a clerical or ministerial capacity.[25] Agents who are administratively appointed by particular insurers normally cease to be licensed as to any insurer if that insurer files a termination of the appointment.[26] An explanation of the reasons for termination may be required[27] and in appropriate cases may result in an administrative or criminal investigation.

EXCESS AND SURPLUS LINES BROKERS

Producers who place business with non-admitted companies under the "excess and surplus lines" laws (see Chapter 12) are usually required to be separately licensed as excess and surplus lines brokers or agents.[28] Obtaining this status may involve different or additional educational or examination requirements, or licensing fees. Excess and surplus lines brokers are also usually subject to fairly stringent recordkeeping and reporting requirements with regard to the business they place with non-admitted companies.[29]

Under some statutes, excess and surplus lines brokers may be expressly required to use "diligence" to ascertain the financial strength and reputation of the companies with whom they place business.[30] Such requirements call attention to the increased financial risk inherently associated with non-admitted companies, and to the fact that such companies' policies are usually not covered by state insurance guaranty funds (see Chapter 13).

REINSURANCE INTERMEDIARIES

In New York, persons who act as intermediaries or "brokers" between ceding companies and reinsurers, or between reinsurers and retrocessionaires, must be qualified and licensed by the regulator.[31] Such intermediaries are subject to examination by the regulator "as often as he may deem it expedient."[32] These licensing and examination requirements are largely the result of a major scandal involving misappropriation of trust funds by certain reinsurance intermediaries in New York and New Jersey during the late 1970's. They appear to reflect a legislative judgment that reinsurance intermediaries warrant special attention due to the large sums of money involved and the potential for manipulation and fraud present in many reinsurance transactions.

The New York statutes and regulations pertaining to reinsurance also require reinsurance treaties to specify, among other things, that the intermediary, if any, is the agent of the reinsurers for the purpose of receiving payments from the cedent and transmitting payments to the cedent.

MANAGING GENERAL AGENTS (MGAs) AND THIRD-PARTY ADMINISTRATORS (TPAs)

A managing general agent ("MGA") can be defined as an agent of a property-casualty company who is authorized to bind risks, issue policies, collect premiums, and, in some cases, adjust and pay claims. ("General agents" in the life insurance field are intermediaries between insurers and "soliciting agents," who actually make sales to the public.) The use of MGAs represents an extreme delegation of authority by the insurer concerned, and is subject to special licensing requirements and other regulatory safeguards in some states.[33] For example, in New York a detailed report must be filed with the insurance department whenever a domestic insurer appoints an MGA in any state, and whenever any insurer appoints an MGA for or in New York. Roughly analogous to MGAs are third-party administrators ("TPAs") who provide administrative services to insurers primarily in the life-health and workers compensation insurance areas. Such TPAs are subject to licensing, examination, and related requirements in some states, including Illinois.[34]

INSURANCE CONSULTANTS; INDEPENDENT AND PUBLIC ADJUSTERS

In some states, persons who engage in the business of providing advice about insurance purchases or related matters must be licensed as insurance consultants.[35] Attorneys, accountants, and other licensed practitioners are commonly exempted from these additional licensing requirements.[36] Independent adjusters, who represent the interests of insurers, and public adjusters, who represent insureds, in connection with the adjustment of property losses, must also be licensed as such in many states.[37]

COMMISSIONS AND REBATING

Most state insurance laws include provisions called "anti-rebating" laws, which state in substance that no insurer, and no agent or broker, may give any money, consideration, or "thing of value" to an insured or prospective insured as an inducement to the purchase of insurance, other than what is stated in the insurance policy or contract, except for items which are worth less than a specified small amount (such as five or ten dollars) and which bear some emblem or other advertising.[38] This kind of prohibition has the primary effect of outlawing rebates of any part of an agent's or broker's commission to that person's customer, in order to obtain a competitive advantage or for any other reason. It also prevents agents and brokers from making business gifts to their customers, except for promotional items of small value. Such provisions, particularly as they apply to insurers, complement the rating laws under which premium rates for many lines of insurance are closely regulated (see Chapter 7), since an insurer could in effect charge less than the lawful rates by giving away money or other property as part of the bargain.

Currently, rebating is apparently not prohibited in the states of California and Florida. The anti-rebating statute was repealed by a provision of California's Proposition 103, a voter initiative enacted in 1988. In Florida, the anti-rebating statute was declared unconstitutional by the state supreme court in 1986.[39] As a practical matter, prohibitions against unfair discrimination in insurance rating practices may continue to deter the practice of rebating in many instances.

REPRESENTATIVE AND FIDUCIARY CAPACITY

The difference between an agent and a broker in the abstract is difficult to define, and in any particular context it usually cannot be determined solely by reference to state insurance laws and the producer's licensing status thereunder. The licensing statutes certainly imply that, in terms of common-law principles, a licensed "agent" generally represents an insurer, and a licensed "broker" generally represents an insured, so that acts done and knowledge obtained by the representative are imputed to the person or entity represented.

A number of states have abolished this distinction by statute as far as the receipt of premiums is concerned, so that even a broker or "producer" may be deemed to be an agent of the insurer, and not of the insured, for the purpose of receiving money from an insured.[40] Beyond this point, however, the statutes do not usually alter common-law doctrines (such as implied authority, apparent authority, and agency by estoppel) under which the issue of agency is largely a matter of facts and circumstances. Therefore, the questions "Whose agent?" and "For what purpose?" must still be answered on a case-by-case basis.

Many state laws also provide that funds (including premiums) held by an agent or broker, on behalf of an insurer or an insured, are held in a fiduciary capacity for the benefit of the insurer or insured, as the case may be, and may not be "commingled" with the agent's or broker's own funds without the principal's consent.[41]

NOTES

1. Rubin, *Dictionary of Insurance Terms* (Hauppague, N.Y.: Barron's Educational Series, Inc., 3rd ed., 1995) p. 25.
2. N.Y. Ins. Law Sec. 2102(b).
3. A broker cannot be licensed for life insurance or annuities in New York. N.Y. Ins. Law Sec. 2104(b)(1).
4. See. e.g., N.Y. Ins. Law Secs. 2103 and 2104.
5. See, e.g., N.Y. Ins. Law Sec. 2103(g)(10) and (11).
6. N.Y. Ins. Law Sec. 2101(a).
7. *Id.*
8. N.Y. Ins. Law Sec. 2101(c).
9. *Id.*
10. See, e.g., N.Y. Ins. Law Sec. 2103(e)(2).
11. See, e.g., N.Y. Ins. Law Sec. 2112(c).
12. Tex. Ins. Code Art. 21.01 et seq.
13. Mich. Ins. Code Sec. 500.1201 et seq.
14. N.J.S.A. 17:22A-1 et seq.
15. Ill. Ins. Code Sec. 490.1 et seq.
16. See, e.g., N.Y. Ins. Law Sec. 2102(a).
17. *Id.* Secs. 2114–2116.
18. *Id.* Sec. 2102(b)(4).
19. N.Y. Ins. Law Sec. 2324.
20. Fla. Ins. Code Sec. 626.011 et seq.
21. See, e.g., N.Y. Ins. Law Sec. 2101(d) and (e).
22. See, e.g., Ill. Ins. Code Sec. 497.2.
23. N.Y. Ins. Law Sec. 2103(j).
24. See, e.g., N.Y. Ins. Law Sec. 2110(a).
25. *Id.* Sec. 2111.

26. *Supra* note 11.
27. See, e.g., N.Y. Ins. Law Sec. 2112(d).
28. *Id.* Sec. 2105.
29. *Id.* Sec. 2118.
30. *Id.* Sec. 2118(a)(1).
31. *Id.* Secs. 2102(a)(1) and 2106.
32. *Id.* Sec. 2106(e).
33. N.Y. Ins. Dept. Regulations, Part 33.
34. Ill. Ins. Code Sec. 511.100 et seq.
35. N.Y. Ins. Law Sec. 2102(a) and (b).
36. *Id.* Sec. 2102(b)(4).
37. See, e.g., N.Y. Ins. Law, Sec. 2108.
38. *Id.* Secs. 2324 (property-casualty) and 4224 (life, accident and health).
39. *Dept. of Ins. v. Dade County Consumer Advocate's Office*, 492 So.2d 1032 (Fla. 1986).
40. See, e.g., N.Y. Ins. Law Sec. 2121.
41. *Id.* Sec. 2120.

11

Holding Companies and Corporate Changes

HOLDING COMPANIES GENERALLY

As discussed in Chapter 4, licensed insurance companies are prohibited under virtually all state insurance laws from engaging in any business other than insurance or certain "incidental" businesses. Conversely, under these laws, no person or business entity can engage in the insurance business without being licensed as an insurance company. Nevertheless, the ownership or control of insurance companies, normally tied to the ownership of stock in the case of a stock insurer, is freely transferable and in recent decades has been accumulating in the hands of "conglomerates" or other holding companies, which as overall enterprises may be engaged in various kinds of businesses.

The rationale behind insurance holding company laws has been stated as follows:

In the past the insurance business existed largely in isolation from the rest of the economy. Companies were engaged only in insurance, and were substantially controlled by their own managements, stock as well as mutual, since stock ownership was generally widely scattered. In this posture, decisions were made for institutional reasons which, more often than not, meant that business was conducted as it had been in the past.

Recently, the walls have been breaking down, both as against the insurers' entry into the rest of the economy through the acquisition of non-insurance subsidiaries and as against the absorption of insurers into diversified holding companies in which other economic interests are often dominant. In such holding company systems, the insurer may be controlled by people who have no sentimental or institutional stake in the insurance business, and will not hesitate to reduce, expand, or otherwise radically alter the shape of that business.[1]

In other words, the rationale for holding company laws is to protect insurers as entities from non-insurance companies, or even individuals, who may acquire control over such insurers through stock ownership or otherwise. The effect of these laws is therefore to extend the scope of "insurance regulation" beyond the regulation of insurance companies themselves. This extension may raise constitutional questions, as discussed below.

REGISTRATION STATEMENTS; REQUIREMENTS

Holding company laws are currently in effect in all states. (See the columns labeled "Holding Companies" in Appendix 3.) The basic requirement usually imposed upon the insurer member or members of a holding company system is the filing of a "registration statement" and amendments with the regulator of the applicable domiciliary state or states.[2] Most holding company statutes do not generally impose registration requirements on foreign insurers, as long as the foreign insurer is subjected to substantially the same kind of requirements (i.e., under a comparable holding company act) under the laws of its state of domicile.[3] The California and New York holding company laws are, however, applicable to certain foreign companies which are considered "commercially domiciled" in those states (because they do a substantial amount of business there).[4]

The registration statement frequently must be filed within 30 days after an insurer becomes "controlled" (as defined in the statute) by a holding company, and its contents usually must include: (1) a copy of the articles of incorporation and bylaws of the holding company; (2) disclosure of the identities of the holding company's principal shareholders, officers, directors, and other "controlled persons"; and (3) information concerning the holding company's capital structure, financial condition, and principal business activities.[5] The registration statement must ordinarily be amended within a relatively short time, such as 30 days, after any material changes in the identity of the holding company or within the holding company system.[6]

ACQUISITION OF CONTROL; REQUIREMENTS

Another fundamental provision of the holding company laws is the requirement that acquisition of "control" of a domestic insurer, usually measured by stock ownership, be approved in advance by the regulator under stated criteria. The basic criterion is whether or not the proposed acquisition is in the public interest, or not contrary to the public interest, of the domiciliary state in question. Under most statutes, "control" is defined as the ability, whether exercised or not, to direct the management of the insurer through the ownership of voting stock or otherwise,[7] and such "control" is presumed to exist if a person owns 10 percent or more of such voting stock.[8]

Anyone who proposes to acquire control of an insurer must provide the regulator with detailed information about the identities of the individual persons and entities involved, and their existing businesses and finances.[9] The acquirer is subject to examination by the regulator as part of the approval process, and there may also be hearings.[10] The various criteria upon which the regulator may base a decision typically include the following: (1) the financial condition of the acquirer and of the insurer to be acquired; (2) the trustworthiness of the acquirer and, if a corporation, of its directors and officers; (3) the proposed plan for conducting the insurer's operations after the acquisition; (4) the source of funds to be used for the acquisition; (5) the fairness of the purchase price or exchange of assets intended as consideration for the acquisition; (6) the effect of the acquisition on competition, including possible monopoly effects; and (7) possible harm or prejudice to the insurer's policyholders or shareholders.[11] Ordinarily the acquisition may not be approved if the acquirer or any of its officers or directors has demonstrated untrustworthiness, or if the effect of the acquisition would be substantially to lessen competition or to tend to create a monopoly.[12]

TRANSACTIONS BETWEEN AND AMONG AFFILIATES

Holding company laws also typically include provisions that regulate transactions between the holding company and the controlled insurance company, and among members of the holding company "system," that is, affiliated insurance or non-insurance companies commonly controlled by the holding company. These provisions normally require that all such transactions be "fair and equitable" or "at arm's length."[13] The rationale for this kind of requirement is that, within a previously approved holding company system, the insurance company or companies should be permanently protected from unfair dealings, such as "raids" on surplus, "sweetheart" contracts, or other improper diversions of assets which could impair its or their solvency. (Of course, the insurance company, as an incorporated entity, normally stands separate and apart from its affiliates as far as solvency and the payment of claims to policyholders are concerned.)

In addition to general requirements that transactions be "fair and equitable," holding company statutes frequently require that charges or fees for services rendered by one affiliate to another be reasonable,[14] and that expenses incurred and payments received be allocated to insurer members of the holding company system on an equitable basis and in accordance with customary accounting standards.[15] Particular proposed transactions between or among affiliates may trigger a requirement that the regulator receive advance written notice and disclosure of all material terms. The regulator may then have authority to disapprove the transaction before it occurs, if it would adversely affect the insurer or its policyholders. Such transactions might include: (1) large purchases, sales, or transfers of assets or investments; (2) reinsurance agreements; and (3) agreements for rendering services, especially such things as agency, general agency, and claim service agreements.[16]

MERGER AND CONSOLIDATION

Just as insurance companies are initially formed and organized under the special provisions of insurance laws, as opposed to general corporation laws, major changes in their structure or operations are also governed by the insurance laws. These major changes include merger, consolidation, and conversion from the stock form of ownership to mutual, or vice versa. As in the general corporation statutes, "merger" means the combination of two entities into one surviving entity, and "consolidation" means a combination into one new entity. Shareholder or policyholder approval by a specified number of votes is normally required.[17] In addition, the plan of merger or consolidation must ordinarily be approved by the regulator or regulators of the state or states involved.[18]

CONVERSION OF FORM OF OWNERSHIP

Conversion of insurers refers to a change from the stock form of ownership to the mutual form, or vice versa. Conversion, especially the "demutualization" of mutual companies by converting them into stock companies, became a relatively popular practice during the 1980's. A fundamental problem in conversions is determining the method or formula by which the value of the old owners' shares is determined and used in transferring those shares to the new owners. A secondary problem is obtaining the approval of the requisite number or percentage of policyholders or shareholders.

Typical requirements for conversion from stock to mutual ownership are: (1) a plan for conversion must be adopted by a majority of the board of directors; (2) the plan must be approved by a majority vote of the shareholders at a meeting called for that purpose; (3) in some cases, the plan must also be approved by a majority vote of policyholders, or of certain policyholders; (4) the plan must specify the price to be paid by the company for its shares, or the price must be subject to the domiciliary regulator's approval before any payment is made; (5) the plan must name trustees to hold the shares in trust until the conversion process has been completed; and (6) the plan must be submitted to the domiciliary regulator and approved as conforming to the statutory requirements and not prejudicial to the company's policyholders or the public.[19]

Typical requirements for conversion from mutual to stock ownership are: (1) application must be made to the domiciliary regulator, pursuant to a resolution adopted by a majority of the company's board of directors, specifying the reasons for the conversion and the ways it is expected to benefit the policyholders and the public; (2) the regulator must conduct an examination of the company and appoint disinterested persons to appraise the fair market value of the company and report to him or her thereon; (3) the regulator must make copies of the examination and appraisal available to the board of directors, after which the board may submit a plan of conversion to the regulator for his or her approval; (4) the plan must provide a basis for exchanging the ownership shares of all eligible policyholders (such as all those who had a policy in force at any time in the past three years) for securities of the converted insurer, or other consideration, or both; (5) the basis of exchange for each policyholder must be determined by an objective formula, such as the amount of premiums received from a policyholder in proportion to all premiums received within a given period; (6) notice of the plan must be given to all current policyholders, a hearing must be held, and the plan must be approved by the regulator as fair and equitable and in the best interests of the policyholders and the public; (7) the plan must be approved by a policyholder vote in accordance with the company's bylaws; and (8) if approved by a specified number of policyholders, such as a majority or even two-thirds, the regulator must issue a new certificate of authority or license, thereby converting the company to stock ownership.[20]

In historical terms, probably the most significant insurer conversions were the mutualizations of several large New York stock insurers following the Armstrong Investigation of 1905, which disclosed extensive mismanagement and waste in the conduct of the companies' operations.[21] Although for many years the New York statute prohibited the demutualization of domestic life insurers, the law was amended in 1988 to permit such conversions, subject to extremely detailed substantive and procedural requirements.[22]

NOTES

1. N.Y. Ins. Dept., *Regulation of Financial Condition of Insurance Companies* (1974), p. 78.
2. See, e.g., N.Y. Ins. Law Sec. 1503.
3. See, e.g., Ill. Ins. Code Sec. 131.13.
4. See N.Y. Ins. Dept. Regulations, Part 80, Sec. 80.2; Cal. Ins. Code Secs. 1215.4 and 1215.13 (definition of ''commercially domiciled insurers'').
5. See N.Y. Ins. Law Sec. 1503(b).
6. *Id.* Sec. 1503(a).
7. *Id.* Sec. 1501(a)(2).
8. *Id.*
9. *Id.* Sec. 1506(a) and (b).
10. *Id.* Secs. 1504(b) and 1506(b).
11. *Id.* Sec. 1506(b).
12. *Id.* Sec. 1506(c)(1).
13. See, e.g., N.Y. Ins. Law Sec. 1505(a)(1).
14. See N.Y. Ins. Law Sec. 1505(a)(2).
15. *Id.* Sec. 1505(a) and (3).
16. *Id.* Sec. 1505(c) and (d).
17. See, e.g., N.Y. Ins. Law Sec. 7104.
18. See N.Y. Ins. Law Sec. 7105.
19. *Id.* Sec. 7302.

20. *Id.* Sec. 7307 (mutual property-casualty companies).

21. See Meyer, *Life and Health Insurance Law* (Rochester, N.Y.: Lawyers Co-operative Pub. Co., 1972, 1995), Sec. 26:3.

22. N.Y. Ins. Law Sec. 7312.

12

Non-Admitted Insurers and Other Risk Management Alternatives

KINDS OF NON-ADMITTED INSURERS

A general rule of state insurance regulation is that an insurance business can be transacted, directly or indirectly, within a given state only by an insurer licensed or "admitted" to do business by that state. Such an insurer is then subjected to regular reporting and examination by that state's insurance regulator, so that the residents of the state are protected from unsound or unscrupulous companies. The exception to this rule is the category of excess and surplus lines, or "non-admitted" insurance (not to be confused with "non-admitted assets," discussed in Chapter 4), which may be defined as insurance transacted by an insurer not licensed in a given jurisdiction.

The non-admitted insurer may be "foreign" (organized under the laws of another United States jurisdiction) or "alien" (organized under the laws of another country).[1] It may be incorporated (that is, an insurance company) or unincorporated, the classic and most important example of unincorporated insurers being Lloyds of London, or more exactly, the "Underwriters at Lloyds." Excess and surplus lines insurance generally includes only commercial property and casualty lines, although certain life-health coverages like disability or accident insurance may be available from Lloyds or other sources and may fall within the scope of excess and surplus lines regulatory laws.

The term "excess and surplus lines" itself is somewhat arcane-sounding and certainly less than self-explanatory. Nevertheless, it is still widely used to the exclusion of the more meaningful term, "non-admitted insurance," or the related but somewhat misleading term, "unauthorized insurance." "Excess and surplus" may, but does not necessarily, denote excess insurance (an amount of liability coverage in excess of the limits of primary insurance) or "surplus" insurance, which presumably means an unusual kind of coverage. It is, however, often referred to in an abbreviated way as "surplus lines," or (perhaps most confusingly) as "excess lines." Another unusual term used in the field of excess and surplus lines is "exportation of risk," which implies placement of a risk with an alien insurer but generally means the placement of a risk with any unauthorized insurer, foreign or alien (i.e., its "exportation" from the state where the insured is located).

PURPOSE AND LEGAL BASIS OF SURPLUS LINES LAWS

The purpose or rationale for non-admitted insurance is basically the same as the rationale for residual markets (see Chapter 9): a potential purchaser's inability to obtain a particular kind or amount of coverage in the usual manner or, more specifically, from the usual market comprised of admitted insurers. This inability may relate to the admitted insurers' capacity vis-à-vis the size of the risk, to the unusual nature or character of the risk itself, or to its extreme "riskiness." For example, a prospective insured may need liability insurance in excess of a very large amount, such as $50 million or $100 million; it may want to insure something very unique, such as an art object or historic building; or it may be in weak financial condition and still want to insure its directors and officers for liability purposes.

The "due process" constitutional principle discussed with regard to licensing in Chapter 3 puts non-admitted foreign and alien insurers outside the regulatory reach of the various non-domiciliary states so long as those insurers do not "transact business" within any state, through representatives or otherwise. (For example, the State of New York cannot prevent a British, German, or even a California-domiciled insurer from entering into an insurance contract with a New York resident, so long as the transaction takes place entirely outside New York.) Therefore, the starting point of excess and surplus lines regulation in a given state is usually a statutory provision that prohibits, with certain exceptions, any person within the state from acting for, or "aiding or abetting," an unauthorized insurer in soliciting, negotiating, or effecting any insurance contract.[2] Among the exceptions is usually one applicable to a special licensee called a "surplus lines broker" or, in a few states, a "surplus lines agent."[3]

GENERAL REQUIREMENTS FOR PLACEMENT OF RISKS

Since non-admitted insurers themselves are almost by definition unregulated, most of the statutory provisions relating to non-admitted insurance focus on the activities of licensed surplus lines brokers. In some states, such as New York,[4] they are actually part of the law regulating agents and brokers rather than comprising a separate "surplus lines" law. These statutory provisions generally fall into four categories: (1) separate licensing requirements, including separate qualifications and fees, for surplus lines brokers (who usually must be licensed as "regular" brokers or agents as well);[5] (2) special application and recordkeeping requirements that fall partly on the insured and partly on the broker with respect to each non-admitted insurance transaction;[6] (3) requirements imposed on the broker to exercise "due care" in the selection of a non-admitted insurer,[7] or to select an insurer only from a "white list" (see the next section); and (4) special premium taxes on non-admitted transactions, payable by the insured or broker [as opposed to regular premium taxes, which are payable by the insurer (see Chapter 16)].[8]

The application requirements usually provide that the insured, the broker, or both, must sign affidavits or sworn statements to the effect that they have made a "diligent effort" to find the required coverage in the admitted market, and have been unsuccessful.[9] The affidavits or statements must then be filed with the regulator,[10] or in some states, such as New York[11] and Illinois,[12] with a special surplus lines "association," which acts as an administrator on behalf of the regulator in receiving and reviewing documentation of surplus lines transactions for compliance. In some states, a diligent effort is automatically "deemed" to be made if a certain number of licensed insurers, such as three, decline to provide the coverage requested.[13] Such declinations may relate to the kind of coverage requested, the amount, or both. The insured is usually required, however, to accept lower limits of coverage from a licensed insurer and to purchase only the unavailable "excess" from a non-admitted insurer.[14] (In this context, excess usually refers to monetary limits of coverage, but it may also refer to certain features of the coverage itself.) The surplus lines broker is usually required to maintain detailed records of all non-admitted transactions for a specified number of years, and to make them available to the regulator for examination upon request.[15]

APPROVED NON-ADMITTED INSURERS

In some states, regulators maintain and publish lists (sometimes called "white lists") of non-admitted insurers who are "approved" to one extent or another.[16] In some of these states, surplus lines brokers may place business only with an approved surplus lines insurer,[17] or with an unapproved insurer only if no approved insurer will accept the risk; in other states, reliance on such an approved status may satisfy or replace the broker's duty to use due care in selecting an insurer. This kind of consideration is particularly important in the event of an insurer insolvency, because non-admitted insurance is invariably not covered by state insurance guaranty funds, and brokers may be exposed to liability to their clients in the event of a non-admitted insurer's insolvency.

New Jersey's requirements for approval or "eligibility" of a non-admitted insurer, which are fairly representative, may be summarized as follows: (1) the insurer must be duly licensed for the applicable kinds of insurance in its state or country of domicile; (2) the regulator must be furnished with copies of the insurer's current financial statements and any other information he or she may require; (3) the insurer must show evidence of "financial integrity" and, if an alien insurer, must maintain a trust account of cash or suitable investments in the United States; (4) the insurer must have a "good reputation" and a management which is not "incompetent or untrustworthy"; and (5) the insurer must not be affiliated with any persons of questionable competence, character, or integrity, or with any foreign government.[18]

NON-REGULATION OF RATES AND FORMS

By its nature, non-admitted insurance is generally not subject to specific regulation as to investments, premium rates or classifications, the form or content of policies, or trade practices in general, even when written by "approved" insurers (although an insurer's reputation and manner of doing business may of course influence the approval process, in accordance with criteria like those summarized above). Many of the laws do, however, prohibit the placement of a surplus lines policy for the purpose of obtaining a lower premium or more favorable terms of coverage.[19] In addition, normally each policy must bear a legend to the effect that (1) the insurer is not licensed in the state in question, and (2) the insured is not covered under the state's guaranty fund (see Chapter 13).[20]

The various statutes regulating excess and surplus lines insurance are identified in the columns labeled "Excess and Surplus Lines" in Appendix 3.

SELF-INSURANCE

The term "self-insurance" is potentially confusing because it has several meanings, some of which differ from its apparent meaning. First, it may mean nothing more than "non-insurance" in the sense that a person or entity voluntarily chooses not to purchase a particular kind of insurance which it might make sense to purchase. For example, a physician who chooses not to carry malpractice insurance is self-insured in the sense that he or she will absorb liability losses directly and entirely, out of savings or other personal assets. This kind of self-insurance is colloquially known as "going bare."

Self-insurance may also refer to a financial plan on the part of a person or entity to fund losses out of personal or corporate assets, such as by the creation of "reserves," or designated assets consciously set aside for the payment of such losses. This kind of self-insurance does not differ very much conceptually from "going bare," except that there is some calculated effort to estimate losses in advance and set aside appropriate funds to facilitate their being absorbed. Self-insurance in a regulatory context normally refers to a program established by a business entity, in conformity with one or more states' statutes or regulations, as a substitute for the purchase of insurance that would otherwise be mandatory. The primary kinds of self-insurance in this context are (1) workers' compensation self-insurance and group self-insurance, and (2) commercial automobile liability self-insurance.

As discussed in Chapter 9, workers' compensation insurance is mandatory in most states, the District of Columbia, and Puerto Rico. An extensive and complicated system of private insurance (both voluntary and assigned risk), governmental insurance (sold by state insurance funds), and self-insurance has developed over the decades since workers' compensation laws were first enacted. Currently, employers are free in most circumstances to choose private insurance, governmental insurance where available, or self-insurance where they can qualify for it, on a state-by-state basis. In other words, for example, an employer with operations in three states (A, B, and C) can be insured by a private insurance company in state A, insured by a state fund in state B, and qualified for self-insurance in state C.

The subject of qualification for workers' compensation self-insurance is usually covered under a particular state's workers' compensation law, rather than under its insurance code or laws. For instance, in New York, the statutes governing workers' compensation self-insurance are found primarily in Section 50 of the Workers' Compensation Law. They basically provide that an employer may satisfy its obligation to insure its workers' compensation liability by furnishing to the Chairman of the Workers' Compensation Board "satisfactory proof" of the employer's financial ability to pay claims for compensation. The "satisfactory proof" must be accompanied by a deposit of cash or securities, or the furnishing of an irrevocable letter of credit or a surety bond, in amounts determined by the Chairman to be necessary, and subject to change from time to time.[21]

Workers' compensation self-insurance is often augmented by the purchase of excess insurance, either voluntarily by employers or as part of the self-insurance qualification process. This excess coverage may be on a "specific" loss basis (in which case the excess carrier pays the excess of any particular claim over the self-insured amount, such as $50,000 to $100,000), or on an "aggregate" loss basis (in which case the carrier pays the excess over a self-insured amount, such as $1,000,000, for all claims incurred in a given period).

Many workers' compensation laws allow for the formation of self-insurance groups, usually consisting of employers within the same industry, or employers engaged in the same activity within a given industry.[22] Ordinarily the group itself, rather than the individual members, becomes liable for the payment of all claims for compensation.[23] In some states, workers' compensation self-insurers are required to participate in a fund, usually called a "self-insurers' insolvency fund," or a similar assessment plan, to pay the claims of employees whose self-insured employers have been unable to do so because of the inadequacy of their deposits, security, and other assets.[24]

Self-insurance for commercial automobile liability risks (commonly defined by statute as those involving 26 or more vehicles) is permitted in many states, and is usually regulated under the provisions of the state motor vehicle law. The risks subject to self-insurance in this context usually include bodily injury as well as property damage liability. For example, in New York, the Commissioner of Motor Vehicles may grant self-insured status under the Financial Security Act (see Chapter 8) to any person having more than 25 vehicles registered, if the Commissioner is satisfied that the person has the "financial ability to respond to judgments obtained against such person, arising out of the ownership, maintenance, use or operation of any such person's motor vehicles."[25]

CAPTIVE INSURERS

Captive insurers are a variation, of sorts, on the concept of self-insurance. A captive insurer can be defined as an insurance company formed for the purpose of insuring only its prospective owners, as an alternative to self-insurance or to the purchase of insurance from commercial or governmental insurers. Captive insurers are typically formed by large industrial and other corporations for reasons of economy, capacity, and tax savings (because premiums paid to captives in some circumstances may be currently tax-deductible business expenses, whereas reserves set aside for self-insured losses usually are not).

A very large part of the captive market involves "off-shore" companies, that is, insurers organized under the laws of foreign jurisdictions such as Bermuda, the Cayman Islands, and Luxembourg. Captives may, however, be organized under the specially designed statutes of several United States jurisdictions, including Vermont[26] (which has the largest number of existing captives), Colorado,[27] Delaware,[28] Georgia,[29] Hawaii,[30] Illinois,[31] Tennessee,[32] and the Virgin Islands.[33]

The basic constitutional principle behind the formation of a captive is that, once formed and licensed in its state of domicile, a captive which restricts its activities to transactions initiated and completed inside that state with its parent or parents cannot (as a matter of "due process") be required to be licensed in any other state. This is true even if the risks to be insured relate to other states, because the captive does not (or at least endeavors not to) "do business" in those other states through the mail, through agents, or otherwise. The statutes which explicitly sanction the formation of captives usually provide further incentives, such as exemption from participation in residual markets and guaranty funds.[34]

"On-shore" captives typically fall into one of three categories, as follows: (1) a "pure captive," which insures only a single parent company and its subsidiaries and affiliates; (2) an "association captive," which is created by, and insures the various members of, a trade association or similar collective enterprise; and (3) an "industrial insured" captive which is controlled by, and insures the members of, an "industrial group" (as defined in the applicable statute).[35] The regulatory controls commonly imposed on captives may include: (1) holding directors' meetings and maintaining a principal office within the state; (2) filing annual reports with the regulator and submitting to periodic examinations; and (3) paying premium taxes, which may be somewhat lower than the taxes imposed on commercial insurers generally.[36]

RISK RETENTION AND PURCHASING GROUPS

As discussed in Chapter 2, the scope of the Federal Product Liability Risk Retention Act of 1981 was expanded by the Risk Retention Amendments of 1986 to include general and professional liability as well as product and completed-operations liability risks. As amended, the law defines "liability" as follows:

(2) "liability"—

(A) means legal liability for damages (including cost of defense, legal costs and fees, and other claims expenses) because of injuries to other persons, damage to their property, or other damage or loss to such other persons resulting from or arising out of—

(i) any business (whether profit or nonprofit), trade, product, services (including professional services), premises, or operations, or

(ii) any activity of any State or local government, or any agency or political subdivision thereof; and

(B) does not include personal risk liability [as defined in the law] and an employer's liability with respect to its employees other than legal liability under the Federal Employers' Liability Act (45 U.S.C. 51 et seq.).[37]

A risk retention group is defined as a corporation or other limited liability company whose primary activity is assuming and spreading the "liability" exposure of its members.[38] The fundamental premise of the law is that risk retention groups are exempted from any state laws or regulations which would generally regulate them or make their operation unlawful, except that (1) the state where the group is chartered may regulate the formation and operation of the group, and (2) any state may require the group to meet certain standards of conduct and to pay premium and other taxes.[39] Several states have enacted legislation that provides for the organization and licensing of risk retention groups,[40] which essentially are captive insurance companies formed under the laws of a United States jurisdiction, or organized and licensed in Bermuda or the Cayman Islands (if that status existed before January 1, 1985).[41]

Purchasing groups, in contrast, are groups composed of members who engage in similar or related business activities and purchase insurance on a group basis to cover their similar or related exposures.[42] Purchasing groups are given an exemption from state regulation similar to the exemption for risk retention groups described above. They are usually "registered" rather than licensed under state law.[43]

NOTES

1. See, e.g., N.Y. Ins. Law Sec. 107(5) and (21).
2. See N.Y. Ins. Law Sec. 2117(a).
3. See, e.g., N.J.S.A. 17:22–6.41(a).
4. N.Y. Ins. Law Sec. 2105.
5. *Id.*
6. See, e.g., N.Y. Ins. Law Sec. 2118(c)(1).
7. *Id.* Sec. 2118(a)(1).
8. Tenn. Ins. Code Sec. 56–14–108(g).
9. See, e.g., N.Y. Ins. Law Sec. 2118(b)(3)(A).
10. See, e.g., Tenn. Ins. Code Sec. 56–14–106(a).
11. N.Y. Ins. Law Sec. 2118(b)(1).
12. Ill. Ins. Code Sec. 445(5).
13. See, e.g., N.Y. Ins. Law Sec. 2118(b)(4).
14. See, e.g., Tenn. Ins. Code Sec. 56–14–108(a).
15. See, e.g., N.J.S.A. 17:22–6.57.
16. See, e.g., Tenn. Ins. Code Sec. 56–14–108(g).
17. *Id.* Sec. 56–14–108(a).
18. N.J.S.A. 17:22–6.45.
19. See N.J.S.A. 17:22–6.43.
20. See, e.g., Ky. Ins. Code Sec. 304.10–090.
21. N.Y. Workers' Compensation Law Sec. 50(3).
22. *Id.* Sec. 50(3-a).
23. *Id.* Subsection (3-a)(2).
24. See N.Y. Workers' Compensation Law Sec. 50(5)(f).
25. N.Y. Vehicle & Traffic Law Sec. 316.
26. Vt. Ins. Code Sec. 6001 et seq.
27. Colo. Ins. Code Sec. 10–6–101 et seq.
28. Del. Ins. Code Sec. 6901 et seq.
29. Ga. Ins. Code Sec. 33–41–1 et seq.
30. Haw. Ins. Code Sec. 431:19–101 et seq.
31. Ill. Ins. Code Sec. 123C–1 et seq.
32. Tenn. Ins. Code Sec. 56–13–101 et seq.
33. V.I. Ins. Code Sec. 1400 et seq.
34. See, e.g., Vt. Ins. Code Sec. 6013.
35. *Id.* Sec. 6001(3), (8), and (12).
36. *Id.* Sec. 6002(b).
37. 15 U.S.C. Sec. 3901(a)(2).
38. *Id.* Sec. 3901(a)(4).
39. *Id.* Sec. 3902(a).
40. See, e.g., Maine Ins. Code Sec. 6091 et seq.
41. 15 U.S.C. Sec. 3901(a)(4); and see Maine Ins. Code Sec. 6093(13).
42. 15 U.S.C. Sec. 3901(a)(5); and see Maine Ins. Code Sec. 6093(11).
43. See Maine Ins. Code Sec. 6098.

13

Insurer Insolvencies and State Guaranty Funds

STATE INSURER INSOLVENCY LAWS; INAPPLICABILITY OF FEDERAL BANKRUPTCY LAW

Although the primary goal of all insurance regulation is the maintenance of insurers' solvency, insurers nevertheless do become insolvent with considerable frequency. For example, there were 372 property-casualty company insolvencies in the United States between 1969 and 1990,[1] and 290 life and health company insolvencies between 1976 and 1991.[2]

The United States Constitution gives Congress the power to make "uniform laws" governing bankruptcy[3] and limits the states' power to make laws that "impair" the obligations of contracts (i.e., laws that provide for the alteration or elimination of existing debts).[4] For these reasons, the United States Bankruptcy Code is normally the only insolvency law applicable to individuals or businesses who seek to have debts "discharged" entirely or restructured through the adoption of a plan of "reorganization." The Bankruptcy Code is, however, expressly inapplicable to insurance companies,[5] as well as to banks and savings institutions[6] by virtue of provisions which state that these kinds of entities cannot be "debtors" under the Code. In the case of insurance companies, applicable insolvency provisions are included in most states' insurance laws, and such provisions are usually referred to as "insolvency" or "liquidation" laws rather than "bankruptcy" laws.

A typical insurer insolvency involves obligations and claimants in more than one state. Multistate aspects of insurer insolvencies are addressed under various states' enactments of the NAIC's model "Insurers Rehabilitation and Liquidation Act." (State insurer insolvency and liquidation laws are identified in the columns labeled "Rehab. and Liquidation" in Appendix 3.) All of the state insolvency laws are technically "non-bankruptcy" laws in the sense that they do not allow for the discharge of insurers' debts, in whole or in part. Therefore, the usual consequence of an insurer insolvency is either (1) rehabilitation involving the elimination of a capital or surplus deficiency through restructuring of debt, a cash infusion, or other methods; or (2) liquidation and dissolution.

The usual features of a state insurance insolvency law are as follows: (1) an insurer is considered to be "insolvent" whenever it does not have sufficient assets to pay all of its obligations as they arise, as indicated by having an excess of liabilities (including reserves) over assets; (2) the insurance commissioner or equivalent officer is authorized or directed to seek appointment by a state court as receiver of the insurer, and in that capacity to take possession of the insurer's business and assets; (3) the receiver may petition the court for an order of liquidation if it appears that rehabilitation of the insurer and the continuation of its business are not possible; (4) in the liquidation, a certain priority of claims is established (with policy claims and obligations sometimes ranking ahead of general debts and obligations, and payment of policy claims being augmented by guaranty funds, as discussed below); (5) certain "preferential" transfers or payments made by the insurer within four months before the insolvency may be recovered by the receiver for the benefit of the insurer's estate; and (6) at the conclusion of the liquidation, the insurer is dissolved and ceases to exist.[7]

The NAIC Insurers Rehabilitation and Liquidation Act establishes nine classes or priorities of claims, which are difficult to summarize briefly but are basically as follows: (1) costs and expenses of administration; (2) administrative expenses of guaranty associations which would otherwise have been incurred by the receiver; (3) policy loss claims, including guaranty association claims; (4) claims of the federal government other than policy loss claims; (5) debts due to employees for services rendered; (6) claims of any person, including state and local governments, other than those which fall into another class; (7) claims of state or local governments for penalties or forfeitures; (8) surplus or contribution notes and similar obligations; and (9) claims of shareholders.[8]

STATE GUARANTY FUNDS GENERALLY

As with insurer insolvency proceedings *per se*, state rather than federal laws govern the functioning of guaranty funds (sometimes called "security" funds) to remedy the effects of insurer insolvencies on members of the public. In general, the state guaranty funds laws provide for payment of limited policy benefits to policyholders of insolvent companies, after the companies' assets have been exhausted. These limited benefits are financed by assessments against all the remaining solvent insurers who are licensed in the jurisdiction in question.

In the case of the banking and thrift industries, the Federal Deposit Insurance Corporation (FDIC) and the Federal Savings and Loan Insurance Corporation (FSLIC) were created in 1933 and 1934, respectively, as a result of the Great Depression, to deal with most insolvencies at the federal level. (The FSLIC was replaced by the Resolution Trust Corporation in 1989.) Insurance company in-solvencies, however, were not the subject of such legislation until the late 1960's, when guaranty fund laws began to be enacted at the individual state level. In general, with respect to an insolvent insurer which has outstanding obligations in various states, the guaranty fund laws of each of those states will be applicable.

PROPERTY-CASUALTY GUARANTY FUNDS

All 50 states and the District of Columbia have enacted state guaranty fund laws to remedy the insolvencies of property-casualty insurers; all states have also enacted life and health insurance guaranty fund laws, as discussed below. (See the columns labeled "P/C Guaranty Fund" and "L/H Guaranty Fund" in Appendix 3.) With the exception of New York, property-casualty guaranty funds generally have the following characteristics: (1) the fund applies to various lines of property-casualty insurance, usually excluding accident and health, title, and ocean marine insurance; (2) each licensed insurer must be a member of the fund (or "association") with respect to certain lines of insurance, as a condition to holding its license with respect to those lines; (3) the fund will be obligated to pay "covered claims" under policies issued by an insolvent licensed insurer where the insured is a resident of the state or the insured property is located in the state; (4) "covered claims" are defined to include first-party and third-party policy claims, usually in excess of a deductible amount (such as $500) up to a maximum amount, which is typically $300,000 (except for the New York law, which has a $1 million maximum), except for workers' compensation claims, to which no deductible and no maximum apply; (5) the funds needed to pay covered claims are obtained as needed by assessments against the membership, based on (a) separate "accounts" for different lines of business (typically three accounts corresponding to automobile, workers' compensation, and "all other" lines), and (b) each member's proportionate premium writings per account in the previous calendar year; and (6) there is a maximum amount (usually 2 percent of written premiums) that the fund can assess against any member for any account in any calendar year.

The New York Property/Casualty Insurance Security Fund[9] differs from all other property-casualty guaranty funds because it is funded by assessments in advance of any particular insolvency. The Fund continues to assess members, even if income exceeds expenditures, until the assets of the Fund equal $150 million.[10] For this reason, the New York Fund is called a "pre-assessment" fund, and all the other property-casualty funds are called "post-assessment" funds. (They probably should be called "pre-insolvency assessment" and "post-insolvency assessment" funds, respectively.) In recent years, the New York Fund has been subjected to borrowing by the State of New York to meet bud-getary needs, with ensuing controversy and litigation over the rights of the in-surer members of the fund to be free from further assessments.

Most property-casualty funds cover claims for unearned premiums[11] as well as loss claims, sometimes subject to a different deductible, a different maximum, or both. A few funds also place limitations on the net worth of entities that may claim benefits from the fund, so that in effect they exclude large commercial policyholders from the scope of their protection. Such a limitation in the Michigan statute[12] was held to be invalid on state and federal constitutional grounds in a 1989 decision by a Michigan federal court.[13]

Property-casualty fund assessments in all states (excluding New York) totalled approximately $5.9 billion from 1969 through 1995.[14]

A few states, including New Jersey[15] and Pennsylvania,[16] have separate guaranty or security funds for workers' compensation insurance. Until 1990, New York had separate stock and mutual workers' compensation security funds, which paid claims of insolvent stock and mutual insurers, respectively, but the two funds were merged in that year.[17] New York still has a separate fund, called the Public Motor Vehicle Liability Security Fund, applicable to policies covering public conveyances, such as taxicabs.[18]

Although, as stated above, a few lines of business such as title and ocean marine insurance are almost always excluded from guaranty fund coverage, workers' compensation claims are almost always covered in full by one fund or another, except in Massachusetts where they were not covered at all until 1989 (but instead were given a priority in liquidation).[19]

LIFE-HEALTH GUARANTY FUNDS

Life and health insurance guarantee funds or associations differ from the property-casualty funds in the following ways: (1) they may apply only to domestic insurers, or to foreign insurers only if the insurer's domiciliary state does not provide substantially similar guaranty fund coverage, or only to the excess over any amount payable by another guaranty fund; (2) they usually provide for indefinite continuation of coverage (by bulk reinsurance or otherwise), in addition to payment of claims and policy cash values, although the premiums or other terms and conditions of coverage may be changed, and there may be moratoriums on the payment of cash values; (3) they frequently contain limits, not only per policy or per coverage, but per life (so that, for example, the total of cash values, disability benefits, and annuity benefits with respect to the same measuring life may be subject to an aggregate maximum, such as $300,000);[20] (4) assessments are usually based upon three accounts corresponding to life insurance, health insurance, and annuities (as each is defined in the statute); (5) assessments may be made in proportion to premiums received by members for each account-line of business over the three-year period before the insolvency; (6) assessments may be based upon insurers' proportionate admitted assets, as opposed to premium writings; and (7) the fund or association may issue "certificates of contribution" to members, and such certificates may quality as admitted assets.

GUARANTY FUND ASSESSMENTS

Within the limits imposed by the guaranty fund laws, losses due to insurer insolvencies, which would otherwise fall on policyholders, beneficiaries, and claimants, are absorbed on a proportionate basis by the remaining solvent insurers. Presumably because of this beneficial effect, many property-casualty rating laws specifically provide that the assessments paid to guaranty funds may be considered in future rate level determinations, so that ultimately these losses may be redistributed to the insurance-buying public in the form of higher premiums.[21] Other states allow a credit for the amount of assessments paid against premium taxes otherwise payable.[22]

NOTES

1. Rejda, G., *Principles of Risk Management and Insurance* (New York: Harper-Collins College Publishers, 5th ed., 1994), p. 592.

2. *Id.*

3. U.S. Const. Art. I, Sec. 8.

4. *Id.* Art. I, Sec. 10.

5. 11 U.S.C. Sec. 109(b)(2) and (3).

6. *Id.*

7. See, e.g., N.Y. Ins. Law Sec. 7401 et seq.

8. NAIC Model Insurers Rehabilitation and Liquidation Act, Sec. 46.

9. N.Y. Ins. Law Sec. 7601 et seq.

10. *Id.* Sec. 7603(c)(1).

11. *Id.* Sec. 7603(a)(1)(H).

12. Mich. Ins. Code Sec. 500.7925(3).

13. *Borman's Inc. v. Michigan Prop. and Cas. Guar. Assn.*, 717 F. Supp. 468 (E.D. Mich. 1989).

14. *1997 Property-Casualty Fact Book* (New York: Insurance Information Institute, 1997), p. 41.

15. See N.J.S.A. 34:15–103 et seq.

16. See 77 P.S. Sec. 1051 et seq.

17. See Practice Commentaries to *McKinney's N.Y. Workers' Compensation Law* (St. Paul, Minn.: West Publishing Co. 1994), Sec. 107.

18. N.Y. Ins. Law Sec. 7604.

19. See Mass. Ins. Law Chap. 175D, Sec. 2, and Chap. 175, Sec. 46A.

20. In New York, the maximum coverage under the Life Insurance Company Guaranty Corporation is $500,000 for life insurance policies. There is no limit for group or blanket accident or health policies. (N.Y. Ins. Law Sec. 7708(a)(3).)

21. See, e.g., Iowa Ins. Code Sec. 515B.13.

22. See, e.g., Kansas Ins. Code Sec. 40–2906a.

14

Reinsurance

REINSURANCE GENERALLY

As discussed in Chapter 5, reinsurance involves a re-transfer of risk (and a commensurate transfer of funds) between or among insurance companies, as distinguished from the initial or "primary" transfer of risk from an insured to an insurance company. Companies are referred to as "cedents" or "ceding companies" when they make such a re-transfer. A company that accepts yet another re-transfer of risk from a reinsurer is called a "retrocessionaire," and the re-transfer is called a "retrocession." The two basic kinds of reinsurance agreement are: (1) an "excess" agreement, under which the reinsurer agrees to pay the excess over a given amount (such as $1 million) on any one loss or on the aggregate losses within a given period; and (2) a "quota share" agreement, under which the reinsurer agrees to pay a percentage (such as 50 percent) of losses.

The business of ceding and accepting insurance is commonly said to be relatively free from regulation, but companies that act as cedents and reinsurers are still engaging in the insurance business and are therefore still subject to regulation in the same fundamental ways as primary insurers with regard to licensing, reports and examinations, and solvency safeguards. In these fundamental respects, reinsurance does not differ very much from primary insurance since the basic functions of assuming and spreading risk are common to both.

AUTHORITY TO CEDE AND ACCEPT REINSURANCE

An insurer is ordinarily authorized to engage in reinsurance, within its state of domicile, as to the same kinds of insurance it is authorized to write directly.[1]

Some states' laws also provide that licensed foreign insurers, or certain kinds of licensed foreign insurers, may reinsure the same kinds of business that they are licensed to insure directly, without any special authorization.[2] Other states do not require foreign insurers to obtain any licensing authority for transacting reinsurance.[3] Illinois happens to have a rather unusual statutory requirement that a domestic insurer must have at least $5 million in surplus, or surplus and capital, in order to accept any amount of certain kinds of reinsurance.[4]

Either expressly[5] or by implication from the laws that allow financial statement credits for reinsurance ceded (see Chapter 5), insurers are normally authorized to cede risks to reinsurers. Furthermore, ceding of some portions of particular risks is required in effect by statutes which specify that an insurer may not expose itself to an ultimate loss (that is, after application of reinsurance proceeds) on any one risk in excess of a certain amount, such as 10 percent of its surplus at any given time.[6]

REINSURANCE AGREEMENTS; INSOLVENCY PROVISIONS

Reinsurance agreements (sometimes called "treaties") are said to be contracts of indemnity, that is, agreements by which reinsurers are bound to reimburse ceding companies for losses incurred and actually paid by the ceding companies. Based on this theory, in 1937 it was held by the United States Supreme Court in the case of *Fidelity & Deposit Co. v. Pink*[7] that a reinsurer was not required to pay reinsurance proceeds to the liquidator of an insolvent ceding company, since the liquidator had not yet paid the losses in question to the policyholders and therefore had no basis to be "indemnified." As a result, the reinsurer experienced a windfall, since it had received reinsurance premiums but did not have to pay the corresponding claims.

In reaction to the *Pink* decision, New York[8] and many other states enacted laws which provide that no financial statement credit for reinsurance ceded is allowed unless the applicable reinsurance agreement contains a clause making the reinsurance proceeds payable to a statutory successor of the ceding company "without diminution on account of the insolvency of the ceding company," or words to the same effect. (See the columns labeled "Credit for Reinsurance" in Appendix 3.) The consequence of such an insolvency clause is that proceeds will be payable, in the event of the cedent's insolvency, to the cedent's liquidator without regard to whether or not the underlying claims have been actually paid.

Policies issued by small or financially troubled companies sometimes contain "cut-through" endorsements, which identify a reinsurer and purport to make the reinsurance proceeds payable directly to the insured in the event of the primary insurer's insolvency. Some state laws, including those of Illinois,[9] appear to validate the use of such endorsements and therefore permit the circumvention of the liquidation proceeding. In at least one case, however, decided by the Supreme Court of Puerto Rico in 1983, it was held that cut-through endorsements violate public policy by preferring some policyholders over others, and are therefore invalid.[10] The use of cut-through endorsements may also be questioned on the grounds that: (1) they might cause the ceding company to lose its financial statement credit for the reinsurance in question, because the cut-through provision conflicts with the required insolvency clause in the applicable treaty; or (2) they might expose the reinsurer to double liability, i.e., to the liquidator and to the insured, if both the treaty's insolvency clause and the endorsement were enforced simultaneously.

FILING AND APPROVAL REQUIREMENTS

Most state laws provide that an insurer must file and obtain the regulator's approval of any reinsurance agreements that pertain to "bulk" reinsurance, or the reinsuring of all or a very substantial part, such as 50 percent, of an insurer's business.[11] These requirements complement the laws governing financial credit for reinsurance (see Chapter 5) and those regulating mergers and consolidations (see Chapter 11). In addition, reinsurance "pools" or "joint underwriting associations" formed by multiple insurers to share risks on a predetermined basis may be required to file their pooling or underwriting agreements with the regulator, at least for informational purposes, in some states.[12] Reinsurance agreements between affiliated members of a holding company system (see Chapter 11) may also be subject to notification or approval requirements under a state's holding company law.

FOREIGN AND ALIEN REINSURERS; CREDIT FOR REINSURANCE

Under New York law and similar laws in other states, the value of reinsurance recoverable by a cedent from a reinsurer is considered an admitted asset (see Chapter 5) only if: (1) the reinsurer is an admitted insurer in the cedent's state of domicile; (2) the reinsurer is an "accredited reinsurer" as determined by the regulator of the cedent's state of domicile; or (3) the reinsurance is supported by a cash deposit ("funds withheld") or other security for the reinsurer's obligations in the event of its insolvency or default for other reasons.[13] New York currently has detailed regulations governing the acceptable forms of security, which include (1) trust agreements under which a qualified bank or other trustee holds the security,[14] and (2) letters of credit under which a bank guarantees payment in the event of a default.[15]

The requirements applicable to trust agreements include the following: (1) the bank trustee must be a member of the Federal Reserve System or a New York state-chartered bank; (2) the assets of the trust must be held in the United States in a form which the beneficiary (i.e., the ceding company) can negotiate without the involvement of the reinsurer; and (3) the beneficiary must have the right to withdraw assets at any time without notice to the reinsurer and without presentation of any statements or documents.[16] The requirements pertaining to letters of credit include the following: (1) the letter generally must be issued by a "qualified bank," as defined in the regulation, and must be presentable and payable at an office of the bank in the United States; (2) the letter must be irrevocable, "clean and unconditional," have a term of at least one year, and contain an "evergreen clause" which prevents its expiration without prior written notice to the beneficiary; and (3) the letter must not be subject to any agreement, condition, or qualification.[17]

"FRONTING"

As discussed in Chapter 4, with regard to direct insurers, most states prohibit any person or entity within the state from assisting an unauthorized insurer in doing an insurance business in the state (except for licensed surplus lines brokers). At least arguably, when an authorized insurer writes a particular kind of business primarily as an accommodation to an unauthorized reinsurer, which in turn accepts all or virtually all of the risk (and premium), the authorized insurer is violating such a prohibition. The term "fronting" is commonly used to describe the function of an authorized insurer that enters into such a reinsurance agreement.[18] The term is difficult to define precisely, but it carries a distinct connotation that the activity in question is subject to challenge as the illegal "aiding and abetting" of an unauthorized insurer. In at least one state (Florida), fronting is defined by statute as the transfer of more than 50 percent of certain risks to an unauthorized and unapproved insurer, and the practice as so defined is generally prohibited without prior regulatory approval.[19]

INSURER INSOLVENCY AND REINSURANCE SETOFFS

Most state insurer insolvency laws (see Chapter 13) contain provisions that allow creditors of an insolvent insurer to claim a right of "setoff" (sometimes interchangeably called "offset") with respect to funds owed by them to the insolvent insurer. A typical instance of such a potential setoff arises under a reinsurance agreement when the cedent owes the reinsurer premium funds, and the reinsurer owes the cedent loss payments. Most insolvency statutes provide that setoff is permissible only in cases of "mutual debts or mutual credits,"[20] but the courts do not always agree on the interpretation of such a "mutuality" requirement.[21] For example, in some cases, it has been argued that the mutuality which exists between a cedent and a reinsurer no longer exists when a new "person," namely a liquidator, takes the place of one of the original parties. (In such cases, it is argued that the requisite "mutuality of capacity" no longer exists.) In a recent California decision,[22] the court rejected such an argument on the basis that the liquidator succeeds to the insurer's rights, subject to the defenses and setoff rights of other parties. The opposite result was reached, however, in a recent New York case,[23] based on the theory that a liquidator acts as a trustee for all claimants and not as a successor to the insolvent insurer.

Another point of contention with regard to setoff rights is the requirement of "mutuality of time," which generally causes debts to be categorized as either pre-insolvency or post-insolvency debts, and allows the setoff only of debts within the same category. This requirement frequently leads to controversy as to when debts arise or "accrue," and to which category they therefore belong.[24]

NOTES

1. See N.Y. Ins. Law Sec. 1114(a).
2. *Id.* Sec. 1114(b).
3. See, e.g., Ill. Ins. Code Sec. 121–2.02.
4. *Id.* Sec. 174.1.
5. See N.Y. Ins. Law Sec. 1308(a)(1).
6. *Id.* Sec. 1115.
7. 302 U.S. 224 (1937).
8. N.Y. Ins. Law Sec. 1308(a)(2).
9. Ill. Ins. Code Sec. 173.3.
10. *Warranty Ass'n of all Kinds v. Commonwealth Ins. Co.*, R-80–334 (P.R. Sup. Ct. 1983).
11. See N.Y. Ins. Law Sec. 1308(e) and (f).
12. See, e.g., Tenn. Ins. Code Sec. 56–5–314.
13. See. N.Y. Ins. Law Sec. 1301(a)(14).
14. N.Y. Ins. Dept. Regulations, Part 126.
15. *Id.*, Part 79.
16. *Supra* note 15, Sec. 126.3.
17. *Supra* note 16, Sec. 79.2.
18. See Gurley, "Regulation of Reinsurance in the United States," 19 *Forum* 72 (Fall 1983).
19. Fla. Ins. Code Sec. 624.404(4).
20. See, e.g., N.Y. Ins. Law Sec. 7427(a).
21. See, generally, Schwab, et al., "Onset of an Offset Revolution: The Application of Set-Offs in Insurance Insolvencies," *Journal of Insurance Regulation*, Vol. 8, No. 4 (June 1990).
22. *Prudential Reinsurance Co. v. Superior Court of Los Angeles County*, 265 Cal. Rptr. 386 (1990).
23. *In the matter of the Liquidation of Midland Ins. Co.*, New York Supreme Ct., N.Y. County, Index No. 41294186 (Slip Opinion, Jan. 31, 1990).
24. Schwab, et al., *supra* note 21 at 501–509.

15

Trade Practices and Miscellaneous Regulations

UNFAIR TRADE PRACTICES AND UNFAIR CLAIMS PRACTICES

As discussed in Chapter 1, the McCarran-Ferguson Act of 1945 exempts the business of insurance from the application of certain federal laws, to the extent that the insurance business is regulated by state law. One of the federal laws in question is the Federal Trade Commission Act (FTC Act),[1] which generally prohibits unfair competition, and unfair or deceptive practices, in interstate commerce. Shortly after the enactment of the McCarran-Ferguson Act, together with the passage of rating laws which again legalized joint rate-making activity (see Chapter 7), many states enacted laws prohibiting unfair and deceptive practices in the insurance business, and thereby suspended the application of the FTC Act and "ousted" the jurisdiction of the Federal Trade Commission over most insurance activity. This historical origin is clearly reflected in the text of most states' trade practices laws themselves. For example, the Illinois statute, which is typical in this respect, begins with the following statement of purpose.

The purpose of this article is to regulate trade practices in the business of insurance in accordance with the intent of Congress as expressed in the Act of Congress of March 9, 1945 (Public Law 15, 79th Congress) [the McCarran-Ferguson Act], by defining, or providing for the determination of, all such practices in this state which constitute unfair methods of competition or unfair or deceptive acts or practices and by prohibiting the trade practices so defined or determined.[2]

The kinds of conduct prohibited by state trade practices laws are usually either defined directly in the laws themselves, or by reference to acts and practices prohibited elsewhere in the applicable state's insurance code, or by a combination of both methods. For example, the Illinois statute quoted above directly prohibits "acts of boycott, coercion or intimidation resulting in or tending to result in unreasonable restraint of, or monopoly in, the business of insurance" and "unfair discrimination between individuals or risks of the same class or of essentially the same hazard and expense element because of the race, color, religion or national origin of such insurance risks or applicants."[3] The statute also prohibits, by reference to other provisions of the insurance code, the following: (1) falsification of an insurer's records; (2) misrepresentation of insurer's assets; (3) improper advertisements of an insurer's financial condition; (4) misrepresentation and defamation generally; (5) rebates of premium or commission; (6) geographical risk declination ("redlining") (see below); (7) discrimination in underwriting as to rates or benefits; (8) unlawful sales inducements; and (9) improper claims practices.[4] The state's insurance regulatory official is usually given authority to conduct examinations and investigations into alleged violations,[5] to hold hearings,[6] and to issue "cease and desist" orders[7] in appropriate cases.

Some state trade practices laws, such as that of Illinois,[8] also prohibit "undefined" practices that are determined by the regulator to be unfair or deceptive, or unfair methods of competition. In such instances, the regulator must ordinarily seek an injunction from a court having jurisdiction,[9] and the court's decision is expressly made subject to further judicial review.[10]

Despite the existence of state unfair trade practices laws and the McCarran-Ferguson Act, the Federal Trade Commission retains the authority to conduct investigations pertaining to the insurance business and to prepare reports of its findings. An important example of such an endeavor was the FTC's study of life insurance costs and benefits in the late 1970's and its sharply critical report of 1979 concerning the subject.[11]

For a number of years, a provision of the California unfair claims practices law[12] was interpreted by the state supreme court as creating a private cause of action for "extracontractual" (or "bad faith") damages.[13] This so-called "Royal Globe" interpretation was abandoned by the California supreme court in a 1988 decision,[14] based on additional analysis of the statute's legislative history and the adverse effects of Royal Globe on the civil justice system, such as excessive jury awards and protracted litigation. The reversal of Royal Globe was not generally applicable to actions which were already pending at the time of the court's decision. Similar issues with regard to private causes of action under unfair claims practices laws have arisen in other states, and the courts have generally found that no such cause of action exists.[15]

GEOGRAPHICAL DISCRIMINATION ("REDLINING")

Many states' insurance codes prohibit insurers from refusing to issue or renew certain kinds of property-casualty coverages, such as fire and personal automobile insurance, solely on the basis of the geographical location of the "risk," [16] meaning the location of the insured property or the insured's residence. Such a prohibition of "redlining," as it is commonly called, is intended primarily to prevent hardship to residents and owners of property in depressed urban areas. In the absence of such laws, some insurers might typically reject all applications for coverage corresponding to a particular ZIP code or other geographical subdivision in underwriting a certain line or lines of insurance.

It is important to recall that under a redlining law, other factors, such as a poor driving record or unsafe conditions of a building, taken together with geographical location, may be a proper basis for declination of coverage, so long as the location is not the sole reason therefor. Special facilities may also be provided for applicants who are rejected for permissible reasons (see the discussion of FAIR Plans and automobile assigned risk plans in Chapter 9).

INSURANCE ADVERTISING

Many states have statutes or regulations dealing with advertising by or on behalf of insurers, particularly in the life insurance and accident-health insurance areas. The basic purpose of these statutes and regulations is, as might be expected, to prevent unfair, misleading, and deceptive advertising. Typical provisions regarding life insurance advertising are the following: (1) "advertising" includes material which is printed, published, recorded, or broadcast; sales literature of all kinds; and prepared sales talks and presentations; (2) the form and content of advertisements must be clear enough to avoid deception, or the capacity or tendency to mislead or deceive, based upon the overall impression created in a person of average education and intelligence; (3) testimonials or endorsements of third parties, whether paid for or not, must be genuine and accurate, and the third party's financial interest in the insurer, if any, must be disclosed; (4) statistics may not be used unless they accurately reflect all relevant facts and their source is disclosed; (5) the identity of the particular insurer, and the particular policy or contract being advertised, if applicable, must be disclosed; and (6) each insurer must maintain a file containing every printed, published, or prepared advertisement, together with a notation as to the manner and extent of its distribution. [17]

Typical requirements regarding accident-health insurance advertising are the following: (1) words such as "full," "complete," and "comprehensive" may not be used to describe coverage in a way which exaggerates the benefits provided; (2) hospital cash benefits may not be described as "extra income" or "tax free," or otherwise described in a way which suggests that they represent a profit; (3) limitations or reductions in coverage, such as waiting periods for coverage of pre-existing conditions, must not be described in a positive manner, such as "benefit builders"; (4) exceptions, reductions, and limitations generally must be disclosed when their omission would have the capacity or tendency to mislead; (5) limitations based on pre-existing conditions must be disclosed in negative terms, with an appropriate definition or description; (6) provisions relating to renewability, cancellability, and termination of coverage must be disclosed in a manner which does not minimize them or make them obscure; and (7) advertisements are subject to the same kinds of rules regarding testimonials, statistics, identity of the insurer, and an advertising file as apply to life insurance advertising (see above).[18]

LIFE INSURANCE REPLACEMENT AND COST DISCLOSURE

In the area of life insurance, most state insurance laws include prohibitions regarding "twisting," which may be defined as improperly inducing an insured or policyholder to drop existing coverage in favor of a supposedly superior, new coverage. (The counterpart to "twisting" in the securities field is "churning," or improperly inducing a stockholder or holder of other securities to make trades primarily in order to generate commissions.) A primary motivation for "twisting" may be, as to an agent or broker, the earning of high first-year commissions, and as to an insurer that deals directly with the public, simply generating new business.

Statutes applicable to "twisting" generally prohibit misrepresentations and false or misleading statements, and in particular they usually prohibit incomplete comparisons of insurance policies or contracts for the purpose of inducing an insured or policyholder to lapse, forfeit, or surrender the policy or contract.[19] Under the authority of such a statute or otherwise, many states have adopted replacement regulations which require certain disclosures and comparisons to be furnished in writing to insureds and policyholders before a replacement transaction can be consummated.

The usual features of such a regulation include the following: (1) "replacement" is defined as including any transaction in which new life insurance is to be purchased, and the proposing agent or insurer knows or should know that existing life insurance will be (a) allowed to lapse, surrendered, or otherwise terminated, (b) converted to another plan of insurance by the use of policy values, or (c) subjected to borrowing of more than 25 percent of the policy loan value; (2) the agent must submit to the insurer, as part of each application, a statement signed by the applicant indicating whether or not a replacement is involved, and a statement signed by the agent to the same effect; (3) the agent must provide the applicant with a prescribed "Notice to Applicant Regarding Replacement of Life Insurance," a completed "Comparative Information Form," and a copy of all sales proposals used, and must also send copies of the foregoing to the insurer; (4) the insurer must verify the information provided to the applicant, correct and notify the applicant of any errors, and send copies of the Comparative Information Form and sales proposals to the existing insurer; (5) the existing insurer, if it chooses to make a "conservation effort," must furnish the policyholder with its own Comparative Information Form and send a copy to the replacing insurer.[20]

The contents of the Comparative Information Form commonly include a description of the coverages, with premiums, cash values, and death benefits illustrated for the next 20 years and at five-year intervals from ages 55 to 95.[21] The "Notice to Applicant" usually contains standardized advice about making meaningful comparisons and about the advantages and disadvantages of replacement in general.[22]

Partly as a result of the Federal Trade Commission's Report of 1979 (see above), many states enacted statutes or adopted regulations dealing with life insurance solicitation and cost disclosure. The usual features of such a statute or regulation are as follows: (1) the insurer must provide to all prospective purchasers a "Buyer's Guide," which contains standardized advice about the purchase of life insurance; and (2) the insurer must also provide a "Policy Summary," which includes a "Statement of Policy Cost and Benefit Information" showing premiums, death benefits, cash surrender values, dividends, policy loan interest rates, and certain "cost indexes" which measure the total cost of the policy with allowances for the time value of money.[23]

PREMIUM FINANCING

Premium financing is a specialized lending business, usually engaged in by specialized finance companies, in which the lender takes a security interest in the unearned premiums under the policies financed, together with a power of attorney which enables the lender to cancel the policy and obtain the unearned premiums if the borrower defaults on the loan payments. Many states have laws that require such lenders to be licensed, set maximum interest rates and charges, and otherwise seek to protect the insured's interests. Regulatory authority rests with the Insurance Department in some states and with the Banking Department in others.[24]

NOTES

1. 15 U.S.C. Sec. 41 et seq.
2. Ill. Ins. Code Sec. 421.
3. *Id.* Sec. 424(3).
4. *Id.* Sec. 424(1) and (4).
5. *Id.* Sec. 425.
6. *Id.* Sec. 426.
7. *Id.* Sec. 427.
8. *Id.* Sec. 429(1).
9. *Id.* Sec. 429(2).
10. *Id.* Sec. 430.
11. Federal Trade Commission, *Life Insurance Cost Disclosure* (Washington, D.C.: U.S. Government Printing Office, 1979).
12. Cal. Ins. Code Sec. 790.03.
13. *Royal Globe Ins. Co. v. Superior Court,* 592 P.2d 329 (1979).

14. *Moradi-Shalal v. Fireman's Fund Ins. Cos.*, 758 P.2d 58 (Cal. 1988).

15. Marema, ''Public Regulation of Insurance Law: Annual Survey,'' XXIV *Tort & Insurance Law Journal* 472, 488 (Winter 1989).

16. See, e.g., N.Y. Ins. Law Sec. 3429.

17. See generally Fla. Dept. of Ins., *Official Rules*, Chap. 4–35.

18. See generally N.J. Admin. Code Sec. 11:1–4 et seq.

19. See, e.g., N.Y. Ins. Law Sec. 2123.

20. See generally Fla. Dept. of Ins., *Official Rules*, Chap. 4–24.

21. *Id.*, Exhibit B.

22. *Id.*, Exhibit A.

23. See generally Fla. Ins. Code Sec. 626.990.

24. See, e.g., N.Y. Banking Law Sec. 554 et seq.; N.J.S.A. 17:16D–1.

16

State and Federal
Taxation of Insurers

TAXATION GENERALLY

The subject of taxation of insurance companies is highly specialized and is not, strictly speaking, part of the subject matter of this text, although in general it may be said that taxation has regulatory as well as income-generating goals. What follows, therefore, is a brief summary of the subject of insurance company taxation, and the reader is urged to consult more specialized texts for further guidance. The related subject of taxation of insurance products, proceeds, and the like is entirely beyond the scope of this text and therefore is not discussed here.

The primary sources of state tax revenues derived from insurance companies are state premium taxes, commonly expressed as flat percentages in the range of 2 to 4 percent. These taxes are usually imposed on insurers based on gross premiums written, net of refunds, during the applicable tax period, except in the case of ocean marine insurance, which may be subject to taxes based on ''underwriting profit.'' Insurers are also subject to corporate franchise taxes in some states, and to local taxes, such as real property taxes, in many states. To the extent that premium taxes are based on a percentage of the cost of insurance and are imposed on the insurer, or ''seller,'' they are analogous to state sales or gross receipts taxes. Provisions for premium taxes payable are included in rate-making formulas or methodologies for most kinds of insurance.

As discussed in Chapter 1, the McCarran-Ferguson Act gives the individual states of the United States the right to regulate the business of insurance; in addition, it expressly gives the states the right to tax the business of insurance.[1] The latter right is not exclusively granted to the states, however, and insurers are subject to federal income taxation in roughly the same ways as other corporations (see below).

There are constitutional limitations on the power of the states to tax insurers, especially foreign insurers, derived primarily from the "due process" and "equal protection" clauses of the Fourteenth Amendment. Shortly after the passage of the McCarran-Ferguson Act, the United States Supreme Court held in *Prudential Insurance Co. of America v. Benjamin*[2] that a state could tax foreign insurers in the absence of a comparable tax on domestic insurers. In 1962, however, the Court decided in *State Board of Insurance et al. v. Todd Shipyards Corp.*[3] that the State of Texas could not impose a tax on policies covering property in Texas where (1) the insurer was not licensed in Texas; (2) it had no offices, employees, or agents in Texas; and (3) the policies were delivered and paid for entirely outside of Texas.

As discussed in Chapter 4, many states impose "retaliatory" licensing requirements on foreign insurers whose states of domicile discriminate against out-of-state insurers. Such requirements may include retaliatory premium taxes, so that state X may automatically tax insurers domiciled in state Z at the rates which state Z imposes on domestic insurers of state X (and vice versa). State premium taxes that discriminate in favor of domestic insurers are of doubtful validity as a result of other Supreme Court decisions. In 1981, the Court held in *Western and Southern Life Insurance Co. v. State Board of Equalization of California*[4] that California's retaliatory tax was valid because it served a legitimate state purpose, namely, the deterrence of other states from enacting and enforcing discriminatory taxes.

In 1985, however, the Court was called on to decide *Metropolitan Life Insurance Co. v. Ward*,[5] in which the insurer challenged certain provisions of Alabama law that imposed significantly higher premium taxes on non-Alabama domestic companies, as compared with the taxes applicable to Alabama domestics, but allowed some reduction in taxes for foreign insurers who had significant investments in Alabama. The Court held that, under the equal protection clause of the Fourteenth Amendment, two of the purposes of the Alabama legislation were improper, namely, the protection of Alabama domestic insurers as such, and the encouragement of insurer investment in Alabama. (The full ramifications of the *Metropolitan* decision are a complex subject in themselves,[6] and it suffices for the purposes of this text to note the decision and its importance in the area of discriminatory premium taxation.)

STATE PREMIUM TAXES

As discussed above, most states impose a premium tax on insurers, based upon a percentage of gross premiums. For example, in New Jersey, stock and mutual companies, both foreign and domestic, are generally subject to the premium tax.[7] As to companies other than life and marine the tax is based on (1) gross premiums, except reinsurance premiums, less (2) return premiums, dividends, and unabsorbed premium deposits.[8] Life companies are taxed on (1) gross premiums, except reinsurance premiums and certain pension and annuity considerations, less (2) premiums returned, dividends and discounts on premiums paid in advance.[9] Marine companies are taxed on an apportioned part of their underwriting profits.[10] The tax is generally at the rate of 2 percent plus 0.1 percent of taxable premiums, except for certain group accident and health policies and legal insurance policies to which a rate of 1 percent plus 0.05 percent is applicable.[11] Marine insurers are taxed at a rate of 5 percent plus 0.25 percent of underwriting profits.[12]

In New York, insurers are subject to (1) a "franchise tax on insurance corporations," generally based on allocated net income,[13] and (2) an "additional franchise tax" based on gross premiums less certain deductions.[14] In California, insurers are subject to a tax for the privilege of doing business in the state, based on either gross premiums, income, or underwriting profit, depending on the kind of insurer.[15] The law provides that these taxes are in lieu of all other taxes except real estate taxes, retaliatory taxes, and certain motor vehicle fees.[16]

As discussed in Chapter 12, premium taxes on excess and surplus lines policies are normally higher than the premium taxes on policies written by admitted insurance companies. For example, in New Jersey, the rate on surplus lines policies in 3 percent.[17] Surplus lines taxes are commonly payable directly by the insured (or by the surplus lines broker) rather than by the insurer.

FEDERAL INCOME TAXES

The federal income taxation of insurance companies is a subject that has been aptly described as "unique and extremely complex."[18] The subject is covered by Subchapter L of the Internal Revenue Code, which consists of three parts: Part I ("Life insurance companies");[19] Part II ("Other insurance companies");[20] and Part III ("Provisions of general application").[21] Basically, an insurer is considered a "life insurance company" if (1) it is an insurance company engaged in issuing life and annuity contracts, and (2) its life insurance reserves, plus unearned premiums and unpaid losses on certain noncancellable policies not included in life insurance reserves, equal more than 50 percent of its total reserves.[22] An insurer that does not meet this test belongs to the category of "other insurance companies" and is taxed differently.

Life insurers are taxed on their "life insurance company taxable income" ("LICTI"), which is equal to (1) "life insurance company gross income" less (2) "general deductions" and a "small life insurance company deduction."[23] The general deductions include deductions for policyholder dividends and for increases in reserves.[24] The regular rates for corporations generally apply to life insurers.[25] Non-life insurers are taxed in basically the same way as non-insurance corporations. Non-life loss reserves must be discounted to a present value.[26] Mutual companies are allowed a generally reduced deduction for policyholder dividends, as compared with stock companies.[27]

NOTES

1. 15 U.S.C. Sec. 1012(a).
2. 328 U.S. 408 (1946).
3. 370 U.S. 451 (1962).
4. 451 U.S. 648 (1981).
5. 470 U.S. 869 (1985).
6. See generally Overstreet and Rubin, "Discriminatory Premium Taxation: A Review of *Metropolitan Life Ins. Co. v. Ward*," Part I, 7 *Journal of Insurance Regulation* 457 (June 1989) and Part II, 8 *Journal of Insurance Regulation* 105 (December 1989).
7. N.J.S.A. 54:18A-1(a).
8. N.J.S.A. 54:18A-4.
9. N.J.S.A. 54:18A-5.
10. N.J.S.A. 54:16–2.
11. N.J.S.A. 54:18A-2(a), 3(a), 2(b), and 3(b).
12. N.J.S.A. 54:16–8a).
13. N.Y. Tax Law Sec. 1501.
14. *Id.* Sec. 1510.
15. Cal. Rev. and Tax Code Sec. 12201 and Cal. Const. Art. XIII Sec. 28(b).
16. Cal. Rev. and Tax Code Sec. 12204 and Cal. Const. Art. XIII Sec. 28(f).
17. N.J.S.A. 17:22–6.64
18. Leimberg et al., *Federal Income Tax Law* (1986), p. 11–23.
19. Internal Revenue Code Secs. 801–818.
20. *Id.* Secs. 831–835.
21. *Id.* Secs. 841–847.
22. *Id.* Sec. 816(a).
23. *Id.* Sec. 804.
24. *Id.* Secs. 807 and 808.
25. *Id.* Sec. 801(a)(1).
26. *Id.* Sec. 832(b)(5).
27. *Id.* Sec. 809.

Afterword: The Future of Insurance Regulation

In its fundamental purposes and methods, which are directed first at maintaining insurer solvency and secondly at the fair and equitable treatment of insurance buyers, the American system of insurance regulation is not much different from its counterparts abroad. There are, however, certain outstanding features of insurance regulation in the United States, which it is hoped this book has illustrated: the extensive non-uniformity which results inevitably from state-level regulation and the perennial tension between federal and state regulatory authority.

A fabric of quasi-uniformity is produced by the "official" functions of the NAIC and secondarily by the centralized awareness of regulatory issues that the NAIC's activities generate. Although it is, at least technically, not a governmental entity but a private association of appointed and elected government officials, the NAIC is much more than a forum for the exchange of information and views, and in many ways it can be thought of as the pratical equivalent of, or a substitute for, a national or federal regulatory agency. From a different perspective, the NAIC may be viewed as an advisory council which has no real power apart from its ability to influence the legislatures of the various states.

The NAIC, and state regulation in general, have been subjected to criticism in recent years, especially with regard to solvency regulation, but as of 1997 there is virtually no force being exerted against the inertia present in the existing system. Barring any unforeseen calamities, such as natural disasters or financial losses leading to the failure of a substantial number of major insurers, uniform or mostly-federal insurance regulation in the United States does not seem likely in the near future. Only in the areas of health care and health insurance does the federal government appear to be occupying the regulatory field to a substantial extent. For example, shortly before this book went to press, Congress enacted the Health Care Portability and Accountability Act of 1996, which amends ERISA and the Internal Revenue Code in ways that constitute a major federal incursion into the regulation of the content of health insurance coverages. It can be expected that there will be further federal incursions, perhaps even to the point of the establishment of some kind of universal health care program in the next century, but such incursions would not necessarily dictate a paramount role for the federal government in regulation of the insurance business generally.

Meanwhile, as of 1997 the NAIC has somewhat deemphasized its state accreditation program and is working on other remedies for problems presented by overlapping and inconsistent state regulation. In terms of legal innovation, it is studying the possibility of using an interstate compact to coordinate state regulatory activities, particularly in the areas of insolvency and guaranty fund operations. Such a compact would entail a partial delegation of state regulatory authority to a central regulatory body or framework. The NAIC is also at work on practical, non-legal solutions to administrative "paperwork" problems in the areas of multi-state agent and broker licensing and rate and form filings. In these areas, the NAIC plans to serve as a central clearinghouse for the various insurance departments, using an electronic data network.

The insurance industry in the United States, as might be expected, is continually becoming more diverse and complex in terms of products, services, and risk management techniques. At the same time there is a trend toward consolidation of American insurers into large national or international businesses, and an increasing presence of non-U.S. insurers in the domestic marketplace. The continued viability of the partly centralized and partly decentralized regulatory system presumably depends upon the degree of sophistication, adaptability, and efficiency it can maintain relative to the nature of the regulated industry itself.

Appendix 1:
Excerpts from the United
States Constitution

ARTICLE I. SECTION 8. The Congress shall have power . . .

To regulate commerce with foreign nations, and among the several states, and with the Indian tribes; . . .

ARTICLE VI.

. . . This constitution, and the laws of the United States which shall be made in pursuance thereof; and all treaties made, or which shall be made under the authority of the United States, shall be the supreme law of the land; and the judges in every state shall be bound thereby, any thing in the constitution or laws of any state to the contrary notwithstanding. . . .

AMENDMENT X.

The powers not delegated to the United States by the Constitution, nor prohibited to it by the States, are reserved to the States respectively, or to the people.

Appendix 2:
McCarran-Ferguson Act
(15 U.S.C. Sec. 1011 et seq.)

SECTION 1

The Congress hereby declares that the continued regulation and taxation by the several States of the business of insurance is in the public interest, and that silence on the part of the Congress shall not be construed to impose any barrier to the regulation or taxation of such business by the several States.

SECTION 2

(a) The business of insurance, and every person engaged therein, shall be subject to the laws of the several States which relate to the regulation or taxation of such business.

(b) No Act of Congress shall be construed to invalidate, impair, or supersede any law enacted by any State for the purpose of regulating the business of insurance, or which imposes a fee or tax upon such business, unless such Act specifically relates to the business of insurance: Provided that after January 1, 1948,* the Act of July 2, 1890, as amended, known as the Sherman Act, and the Act of October 15, 1914, as amended, known as the Clayton Act, and the Act of September 26, 1914, known as the Federal Trade Commission Act, as amended, shall be applicable to the business of insurance to the extent that such business is not regulated by State law.

SECTION 3

(a) Until January 1, 1948,* the Act of July 2, 1890, as amended, known as the

*Changed to June 30, 1948, by the Act of July 25, 1947.

Sherman Act, and the Act of October 15, 1914, as amended, known as the Clayton Act, and the Act of September 26, 1914, known as the Federal Trade Commission Act, and the Act of June 19, 1936, known as the Federal Trade Commission Act, shall not apply to the business of insurance or to acts in the conduct thereof.

(b) Nothing contained in this Act shall render the said Sherman Act inapplicable to any agreement to boycott, coerce, or intimidate, or act of boycott, coercion, or intimidation.

SECTION 4

Nothing contained in this Act shall be construed to affect in any manner the application to the business of insurance of the Act of July 5, 1935, as amended, known as the National Labor Relations Act, or the Act of June 25, 1938, as amended, known as the Fair Labor Standards Act of 1938, or the Act of June 5, 1920, known as the Merchant Marine Act, 1920.

SECTION 5

As used in this Act, the term ''State'' includes the several States, Alaska, Hawaii, Puerto Rico, Guam, and the District of Columbia.

SECTION 6

If any provision of this Act, or the application of such provision to any person or circumstances, shall be held invalid, the remainder of the Act, and the application of such provision to persons or circumstances other than those as to which it is held invalid, shall not be affected.

Appendix 3:
Table of Key Statutory Provisions

Appendix 3

STATE/ TERRITORY	Insurance Comm'r	Annual Statements	Examina- tions	Admitted Assets	Investments
AL	27-2-2 +	27-3-26	23-2-21	27-31-1	27-41-1+
AK	21.06.010 +	21.09.200	21.06.120	21.18.010	21.21.010
AZ	20.141+	20-223	20-156+	20-501	20-537+
AR	23-61-102+	23-63-216	23-61-201+	23-63-601	23-63-801+
CA	12900+	900	730+	1153	1170+
CO	10-1-104+	10-3-109	10-1-110	10-1-102(1)	10-3-213+
CT	38-3+	38-24	38-7	–	38-144+
DE	302+	526	322+	1101-1102	1301+
DC	35-101+	35-103+	35-418	–	35-634+ 35-1521
FL	624.302+	624.424	624.316	625.012+	625.301+
GA	33--2-1+	33-3-21+	33-2-11	33-101+	33-1-1+
HI	431:2-103+	431:3-301	431:3-302	431:5-201	431:6-101
ID	41-202+	41-335	41-219+	41-601+	41-701+
IL	401+	136	132	3.1	124+
IN	27-1-1-2	27-1-20-21+	27-1-3-8	–	27-1-12-2 27-1-13-3
IA	505.2+	508.11 515.63	507.1	–	511.8 515.35
KS	40-103	40-225	40-222	–	40-2a01, 2b01
KY	304.2-020	304.3-240	304.2-210	304.6-010	304.7-010
LA	22:2	22:161	22:1301+	–	22:841+
ME (Title 24-A)	201+	423	221	901+	1101+
MD (Art. 48A)	15+	58	30+	75+	86+, 97+
MA	175:3A	175:25	175:4	–	175:63
MI	500.202+	500.438	500.222+	–	500.901+
MN	60A.03	60A.13	60A.031	60A.12	60A.11, 61A.28
MS	83-1-3+	83-5-55	83-1-25+	–	83-19-51+
MO	374.020	379.105 376.350	374.110	375.325+	376.300

(+ = et seq.)

STATE/ TERRITORY	Insurance Comm'r	Annual Statements	Examina- tions	Admitted Assets	Investments
MT	33-1-301	33-2-701	33-1-401	33-2-501+	33-2-501+
NE	44-101.01	44-322	44-107e	44-414	44-309+
NV	679B.020	680A.270	679B.230	681B.010+	682A.010+
NH	400-A:1	400-A:36	400-A:37	–	411-A:1
NJ	17:1C-3	17:23-1	17:23-4+	–	17:24-1+ 17B:20-1+
NM	59A-2-1	59A-5-29	59A-4-5	59A-8-1+	59A-9-1+
NY	201+	307, 4233	309+	1301+	1401+
NC	58-2-5+	58-2-165	58-2-130	–	58-7-85 58-7-90
ND	26.1-01-01+	26.1-03-07	26.1-03-19	–	26.1-05-08+
OH	3901.011+	3907.19 3927.08	3901.07	–	3907.14 3925.05+
OK	302+	311	308+	1501+	1601+
OR	731.236	731.574	731.300	733.010+	733.510+
PA (Title 40)	42	443	51+	–	504.1+
PR	201+	331	214	501+	601+
RI		27-12-1	27-1-11 27-2-19	–	27-11-1 27-11.1-1
SC	38-3-60	38-13-80	38-13-10	–	38-11-10 +
SD	58-2-2.1+	58-6-75	58-3-1+	58-26-1+	58-27-1+
TN	56-1-201+		56-1-408 56-1-410	56-1-405	56-3-301+ 56-3-401+
TX					
UT	31A-2-102+	31A-4-113	31A-2-203	31A-17-201+	31A-18-105+
VT		3561	3563 +	–	3461
VI	53	222	101	501+	551+
VA	38.2-200	38.2-1300 +	38.2-1317 +	38.2-1403	38.2-1400 +
WA	48.02.010 +	48.05.250	48.03.010 +	48.12.010 +	48.13.010 +
WV	33-2-1+	33-4-14	33-2-9	33-7-1+	33-8-1+
WI	601.41+		601.43	–	620.22 +
WY	25-2-102 +	26-3-123	26-2-116 +	26-6-101+	26-7-101+

STATE/ TERRITORY	Separate Accounts	Credit for Reinsurance	Lines of Insurance	Rates/ Rating Organizations	Std. Nonfor- feiture Law
AL	27-38-1+	27-5-12	27-5-1 +	27-13-20 + 27-13-60	27-15-28
AK	21.42.370	21.12.020	21.12.030	21.39.010	21.45.300
AZ	20-536.01	20-261	20-251+	20-341, 20-381	20-1231
AR	23-81-401 +	23-62-204	23-62-101+	23-67-101+	23-81-201
CA	10506 +	922.2 +	100 +	1850.4 +	10159
CO	10-7-401+	10-3-118	10-3-102	10-4-401+	10-7-301+
CT	38-33a		38-93	38-201a +	38-130b +
DE	2932	910	901+	2501+	2929
DC	35-639	35-635	35-1403 35-1514	35-1601 35-1701	35-507
FL	627.802+	624.610	624.601+	627.011+	627.476
GA	33-11-34+	33-7-14	33-3-5	33-9-1+	33-25-4
HI	431:6-323	431:5-306	431:1-203	431:14-101+	431:10D-104
ID	41-1936+	41-511	41-501+	41-1401+ 41-1601+	41-1927
IL	245.21+	173+	4	–	229.2
IN	27-1-12-2.5	27-6-1.1-3	27-1-5-1	27-1-22-1+	27-1-12-7
IA	508.A1+	515.49	515.48	515.A1+	508.37
KS	40-436	40-212	40-401 40-1102	40-925+ 40-1111	40-428
KY	304.15-390	304.5-140	304.5-010+	304.13-011+	304.15-300+
LA	22:1500	22:941+	22:6	22:1401	22:168
ME (Title 24-A)	2537	731	701+	2301+	2528+
MD (Art. 48A)	96A	74	63+	241+, 244+	414
MA	175:132G	175:47	175:47	174A:1+ 175A:1+	175:144
MI	500.925	–	500.600+	500.2301+ 500.2400+ 500.2600+	500.4060+
MN	61A:14 61A.275	60A.09	60A.06	70A.01	61A.24

STATE/ TERRITORY	Separate Accounts	Credit for Reinsurance	Lines of Insurance	Rates/ Rating Organizations	Std. Nonfor-feiture Law
MS	83-7-27	83-19-71	83-31-11	83-2-1+	83-7-25
MO	376.309	375.246	379.010	379.316, 420	379.630
MT	33-20-601+	33-2-1205	33-1-206+	33-16-101+	33-20-201+
NE	44-402.01	44-416.01	44-201	44-1401+	44-407
NV	688A.390	681A.110	681A.010+	686B.010+	688A.290+
NH	408:23+	405:45+	404:1+	412:8+ 412:14+ 413:1+, 414:1+	409:1+
NJ	17B:28-1+	–	17:17-1	17:29A-1+	17B:25-19
NM	59A-20-30	59A-7-11	59A-7-1+	59A-17-1+	59A-20-31
NY	4240	1308	1113	2301+	4221+
NC	58-7-95	58-7-20	58-7-15	58-36-1+ 58-40-1	58-58-55
ND	26.1-33-13	26.1-02-21	26.1-05-02, 03 26.1-12-11	26.1-25-01+	26.1-33-18
OH	3907.15	–	3929.01	3935.01+	3915.07
OK	–	711+	701+	900.1+	4029
OR	733.220	731.508	731.150+	737.007+	743.204+
PA (Title 40)	506.2	442.1	382	1181+, 1221+	510.1
PR	1329+	412, 511	401+	1201+	1328
RI	27-32-1	–	27-8-1	27-6-1 27-7.1-3+ 27-9-1+	27-4-13.1
SC	38-67-10	38-5-60 38-9-190	38-5-30	38-73-10+	38-63-510+
SD	58-28-13+	58-14-1+	58-9-1+	58-24-1+	58-15-43
TN	56-3-501	56-2-208	56-2-201	56-5-301+	56-7-401
TX	3.75	5.75-1	3.01, 8.01	5.01+	3.44a
UT	31A-5-217	31A-17-404	31A-1-301	31A-19-101+	31A-22-408
VT	3855+	3634	3301	4681+	3741+
VI	–	514	451+	–	984

STATE/ TERRITORY	Separate Accounts	Credit for Reinsurance	Lines of Insurance	Rates/ Rating Organizations	Std. Nonforfeiture Law
VA	38.2-3113	38.2-1316	38.2-101+	38.2-1900+ 38.2-2000+	38.2-3200+
WA	48.18A.020	48.12.160	48.11.020+	48.19.010+	48.76.010+
WV	33-13A-1+	33-4-15	33-1-10	33-20-1+	33-13-30
WI	620.02	627.23	–	625.01+ 626.02+	632.43
WY	26-16-502	26-5-111	26-5-101+	26-14-101+	26-16-201+

STATE/ TERRITORY	Std. Valuation Law	Group Life Ins. Definition	Holding Companies	Excess and Surplus Lines	Agent/Broker Licensing
AL	27-36-7	27-18-15	27-29-1	27-10-20+	27-7-1+, 27-8-1+
AK	21.18.110	21.48.010	21.22.010	21.34.010+	21.27.010+
AZ	20-510	20-1251+	20-481	20-407	20-281+
AR	23-84-101+	23-83-101+	23-63-501	23-65-301	23-64-201+
CA	10489.1+	10201+	1215+	1760+	1621+
CO	10-7-301+	10-7-201	10-3-801+	10-5-101+	10-2-201+
CT	38-130b+	38-153	38-39g+	38-78+	38-69+
DE	1111+	3101+	5001+	1901+	1701+
DC	35-501	35-514	35-2001+	35-1544	35-425
FL	625.121	627.551	628.804	626.913	626.011
GA	33-10-13	33-27-1	33-13-1	33-5-20+	33-23-1+
HI	431:5-307	431:10D-201+	431:11-101+	431:8-300+	431:9-101+
ID	41-612	41-2002+	41-3801+	41-1211+	41-1020+
IL	223	230.1	131.1+	445+	490.1+
IN	27-1-12-10	27-1-12-37	27-1-23-1+	27-1-15.5-5	27-1-15.5-1+
IA	508.36	509.1	521A.1+	515.147+	522.1+
KS	40-409	40-433	40-3301+	40-246b+	40-239+ 40-3701+
KY	304.6-120+	304.16-020+	304.37-010+	304.10-010+	304.9-010+
LA	22:163	22:175	–	22:1260	22:1111, 22:1161
ME (Title 24A)	951	2601+	222	2001+	1501+
MD (Art. 48A)	83	417+	491+	183+	165+
MA	175:9	175:133	175:193L+	175:168	175:162+
MI	500.832	500.4400+	500.1301+	500.1901+	500.1200+
MN	61A.25	61A.09	60D.01+	60A.195+	60A.17+
MS	83-7-23	–	83-6-1+	83-21-17+	83-17-1+
MO	376.370+	376.691	382.010+	384.011+	375.012+
MT	33-2-521+	33-20-1101	33-2-1101+	33-2-301+	33-17-101+

STATE/ TERRITORY	Std. Valuation Law	Group Life Ins. Definition	Holding Com- panies	Excess and Surplus Lines	Agent/Broker Licensing
NE	44-404	44-1601+	44-2101+	44-139+	44-4001+
NV	681B.110+	688B.010+	692C.010+	685A.010+	683A.010+
NH	410:1+	408:15+	401-B:1	405:24+	402:15
NJ	17B:19-8	17B:27-1+	17:27A-1+	17:22-6.40+	17:22A-1+
NM	59A-8.5+	59A-21-1+	59A-37-1+	59A-14-1+	59A-12-1+
NY	4217+	4216+	1501+	2118, 2130	2101+
NC	58-58-50	58-58-135	58-19-1+	58-28-1+	58-33-1+
ND	26.1-35-01+	–	26.1-10-01+	26.1-44-01+	26.1-26-01+
OH	3903.72	3917.01	3901.31+	3905.30+	3905.01+
OK	1510	4101	1651+	1108+	1421+
OR	733.110+	743.348	732.605	735.400	744.001+
PA (Title 40)	71+	532.1	459.6+	1006.1+	231+
PR	510	1401	–	1007+	901+
RI	27-4-17	–	27-35-1+	27-3-38+	27-3-1+
SC	38-9-180	38-65-40	38-21-10+	38-45-10+	38-43-10+
SD	58-26-21+	58-16-1+	58-5A-1+	58-32-1+	58-30-1+
TN	56-1-403	–	56-11-201	56-14-101	56-6-131+
TX	3.28	3.50	21.49-1	1.14-2	21.07
UT	31A-17-403	31A-22-501+	31A-16-101+	31A-15-103+	31A-23-101+
VT	3781+	3801+	3681+	5023+	4791+
VI	513	–	–	653+	751+
VA	38.2-3126+	38.2-3320	38.2-1322+	38.2-4800+	38.2-1800+
WA	48.74.010+	48.24.010+	48.31A.005+	48.15.040+	48.17.010+
WV	33-7-9+	33-14-1+	33-27-1+	33-12-10+	33-12-1+
WI	623.06	632.55	617.01+	618.41+	628.03+
WY	26-6-201+	26-17-101+	–	26-11-101+	26-9-101+

STATE/ TERRITORY	Unfair Trade Practices	Premium Financing	Rehab. and Liquidation	P/C Guaranty Fund	L/H Guaranty Fund
AL	27-12-1+	27-40-1+	27-32-1+	27-42-1+	27-44-1+
AK	21.36.010+	06.40.010+	21.78.010+	21.80.010+	
AZ	20-441+	20-2001+	20-611+	20-661+	20-681+
AR	23-66-201+		23-68-101+	23-90-101+	23-96-101+
CA	790+	778+	1010+	1063+	
CO	10-3-1101+		10-3-401+, 501	10-4-501+	
CT	38-60+	38-290+	38-421+	38-273+	38-301+
DE	2301+	4801+	5901+	4201+	4401+
DC	35-518	35-1551+	35-419+	35-1901	
FL	626.951+	627.826+	631.001+	635.50+	631.711+
GA	33-6-1+	33-22-1+	33-37-1+	33-36-1+	33-38-1+
HI	431:13-101+	–	431:15-101+	431:16-101+	431:16-201
ID	41-1301+	–	41-3301+	41-3601+	41-4301+
IL	421+	513+	187+	532+	531.01+
IN	27-4-1-1+		27-9-1-1+	27-6-8-1+	27-8-8-1+
IA	507B.1+	–	507C.1+	515B.1+	508C.1+
KS	40-4201+	40-2601+	40-3601+	40-2901+	40-3001+
KY	304.12-010+	304.30-010+	304.33-010+	304.36-010+	304.42-010+
LA	22:1211+		22:733+, 757	22:1375	–
ME (Title 24-A)	2151+		4351+, 4363	4431	4601
MD (Art. 48A)	212+	486+	132+, 152	504+	520+
MA	176D:1+		175:180A+	175D:1+	175:146B
MI	500.2001+	500.1501+	500.8101+	500.7901+	500.7701+
MN	72A.17+	59A.01+	60B.01+	60C.01+	61B.01+
MS	83-5-29+	–	83-23-1+	83-23-101+	83-23-201+
MO	375.930+	–	375.950+	375.771+	376.715
MT	33-18-101+	33-14-101+	33-2-1301+	33-10-101+	33-10-201+
NE	44-1522+	–	44-4801+	44-4201+	44-2701+

STATE/ TERRITORY	Unfair Trade Practices	Premium Financing	Rehab. and Liquidation	P/C Guaranty Fund	L/H Guaranty Fund
NV	686A.010+	686A.330+	696B.010+	687A.010+	686C.010+
NH	417:1+	415-B:1+	402-C:1+	404-B:1+	404-D:1+
NJ	17:29B-1+	17:16D-1+	17:30C-1+ 17B:32-1+	17:30A-1+	
NM	59A-16-1+	59A-45-1+	59A-41-1+ 59A-41-17+	59A-43-1+	59A-42-1+
NY	2401+, 2601+	Banking Law Sec. 554+	7401+	7601+	7701+
NC	58-63-1+	58-35-1+	58-30-1+	58-48-1+	58-62-1+
ND	26.1-04-03+	26.1-20.1-01+	26.1-07-08+	26.1-42-01+	26.1-38.1-01+
OH	3901.19+	1321.71	3903.01+	3955.01+	3956.01+
OK	1201+	–	1801+, 1901+	2001+	2021+
OR	746.005+	746.405+	734.010+	734.510+	734.750+
PA (Title 40)	1171.1+	3301+	221.1+	1701.101+	1801
PR	2701+	–	4001+	3801+	3901+
RI	27-29-1+	27-40-1+	27-14-1+	27-34-1+	27-34.1-1+
SC	38-57-10+	38-39-10+	38-27-10+	38-31-10	38-29-10
SD	58-33-1	–	58-29B-1+	58-29A-1+	58-29C-1+
TN	56-8-101+	56-37-101+	56-9-101+	56-12-101+	56-12-201+
TX	21.21+	24.01+	21.28+	21.28-C	21.28-D
UT	31A-26-303	31A-21-305	31A-27-101+	31A-28-201+	31A-28-101+
VT	3861	7001+	3591+	3611+	4151+
VI	1201+	–	1253+ 1261+	231+	–
VA	38.2-500+	38.2-4700+	38.2-1500+	38.2-1600+	38.2-1700+
WA	48.30.010+	48.56.010+	48.31.110	48.32.010+	48.32A.010+
WV	33-11-1+	–	33-10-1+	33-26-1+	33-26A-1+
WI	628.34	–	645.01+	646.01+	646.01+
WY	26-13-101+	–	26-28-101 26-28-119	26-31-101+	26-42-101+

Glossary

accredited reinsurer: A non-admitted foreign or alien insurer which is approved by the insurance regulatory authorities of a given state for the purpose of allowing the ceding company to take credit for the reinsurance on its annual statement.

admitted asset: An asset of an insurer for which it is legally allowed to take credit on its annual statement.

admitted insurer: A foreign or alien insurer licensed to do business in a given jurisdiction.

advisory organization: A cooperative enterprise of insurers which collects statistics and recommends rates, policy forms, and the like to its members.

agent: A representative of an insurer who deals with purchasers of insurance.

AIPSO: See Automobile Insurance Plans Service Office.

alien insurer: An insurer organized under the laws of a country other than the United States.

amortized value: The value of a bond or similar investment security, used on an insurer's annual statement, and based on the yield and ultimate maturity value rather than market value.

ancillary receiver: An assistant receiver for an insolvent insurer, appointed under the laws of a state other than the insurer's state of domicile. *See also* domiciliary receiver and receiver.

annual report: See annual statement.

annual statement: A detailed financial report which must be furnished annually by every insurer to the insurance regulatory authorities of the states where it is licensed.

anti-rebating law: A state law which prohibits insurers and insurance agents and brokers from giving back any part of a premium or commission to an insured.

antitrust law: A state or federal law which prohibits various kinds of anti-competitive business behavior, such as monopolies.

assigned risk plan: A voluntary or mandatory arrangement under which licensed insurers share proportionately in providing necessary kinds of insurance to applicants who are unable to obtain them otherwise.

Automobile Insurance Plans Service Office (AIPSO): An insurance industry organization which administers automobile assigned risk plans, collects statistics, and develops rates for the automobile assigned risk market.

basket provision: Part of the investment laws of a given state which allows insurers to invest a relatively small percentage of their assets without regard to the usual legal restrictions. Also called leeway provision.

Best rating: A financial rating (such as A or B+) of an insurer issued by A.M. Best & Co., similar to a Moody's or Standard & Poor's rating.

Blanks Committee: A committee or task force of the National Association of Insurance Commissioners (NAIC) which recommends changes in the standard form of annual statement (also called the Convention Blank). *See also* National Association of Insurance Commissioners.

blue book: A life-health insurer's annual statement, the cover of which is usually blue. *See also* annual statement *and* yellow book.

Blues: Blue Cross and Blue Shield organizations, usually organized and licensed as non-profit health insurers.

broker: A representative of a purchaser of insurance who deals on the purchaser's behalf with insurers.

bulk reinsurance: The ceding of all or a substantial part of an insurer's business to a reinsurer.

cancellation: Termination of an insurance policy, at the election of the insurer or the insured, before its normal expiration date.

captive insurer: An insurer formed primarily for the purpose of insuring its owner or owners.

cash surrender value: See policy cash surrender value.

casualty insurance: Insurance against legal liability based upon negligence and the like. Usually synonymous with liability insurance.

certificate of group insurance: A relatively brief written summary of the coverages provided to members of a group under a group life, accident, or health insurance policy or a group annuity contract.

certificate of insurance: Written evidence of one or more property-casualty coverages, provided by the insurer or its representative and typically given by the insured to a third party, such as a landlord or mortgagee.

classification system: A system for classifying property and casualty risks (insureds) for premium rating purposes according to their respective risk factors.

Clayton Act: A federal antitrust law which prohibits, among other things, business combinations and mergers which restrain competition.

COBRA: See Consolidated Omnibus Budget Reconciliation Act.

Commerce Clause: Part of the United States Constitution which authorizes the federal government to regulate interstate commerce.

competitive rating: A system of property-casualty insurance pricing, established by statute in some states, under which insurers develop their rates independently rather than through a rating organization. *See also* rating organization.

conformity-to-statute provision: A provision in an insurance policy which states that the policy automatically includes all legally required provisions.

consent-to-rate agreement: An agreement between an insurer and insured, authorized by state law, under which rates higher than the filed and approved rates may be used.

Consolidated Omnibus Budget Reconciliation Act (COBRA): A federal law enacted in 1985, part of which requires continuation of group health insurance coverages in certain instances.

convention blank: The standard form of life-health or fire-casualty insurer's annual statement adopted by the National Association of Insurance Commissioners. *See also* National Association of Insurance Commissioners.

conversion of form of ownership: Change in an insurer's form of ownership, usually from stock to mutual or vice versa.

conversion of group coverage: A change from group life or health coverage to individual coverage, at the election of the person insured.

countersignature requirement: A statute which requires that a resident insurance agent or broker sign a policy issued through a non-resident agent or broker.

cut-through endorsement: An endorsement on a property-casualty policy which provides that a named reinsurer will pay claims directly if the direct insurer becomes insolvent.

deemer provision: A provision of an insurance code which states that a filing of proposed rates or forms will be deemed approved by the regulator if not affirmatively disapproved within a prescribed time period.

demutualization: Conversion of an insurer from mutual ownership to stock ownership. *See also* mutualization.

deposits: See statutory deposits.

deviation: The legally permitted use of rates which are higher or lower (usually by a uniform percentage) than the rates filed by a rating organization for its members.

direct insurer: The insurer directly obligated to the insured or claimant, as opposed to a reinsurer.

dividend: See policy dividend *and* stock dividend.

domestic insurer: An insurer incorporated or organized under the laws of a given jurisdiction, such as the State of New York. *See also* foreign insurer *and* alien insurer.

domicile: The state or other jurisdiction under whose laws an insurer is incorporated or organized.

domiciliary receiver: The receiver for an insolvent insurer appointed under the laws of the insurer's state of domicile. *See also* ancillary receiver *and* receiver.

early warning system: See Insurance Regulatory Information System.

earned premium: The portion of an annual or other periodic premium which has been "earned" by the insurer due to the passage of time and is therefore not refundable in the event the policy is terminated. *See also* unearned premium.

eligible surplus lines insurer: A non-admitted insurer which has been approved by the regulatory authorities of a given state for the issuance of excess and surplus lines coverages. *See also* excess and surplus lines *and* white list.

Employee Retirement Income Security Act (ERISA): A complex federal law, enacted in 1974, which regulates pension plans and other employee benefits.

entire contract clause: A provision in an insurance policy which states that the policy contains the entire agreement between the insurer and insured.

ERISA: See Employee Retirement Income Security Act.

excess and surplus lines: Property-casualty insurance coverages which are sold under special statutory conditions, by non-admitted insurers, usually for large or unusual risks. *See also* surplus lines.

exportation of risk: Issuance of a policy on a risk in a given state by a non-admitted excess and surplus lines insurer. *See also* excess and surplus lines.

Fair Access to Insurance Requirements (FAIR) Plan: A plan, usually mandated by statute, under which licensed insurers share in providing fire and other hazard insurance to property owners who cannot obtain it otherwise.

FAIR Plan: See Fair Access to Insurance Requirements Plan.

Federal Trade Commission Act: A federal law which prohibits unfair methods of competition and unfair or deceptive trade practices.

fictitious groups: Groups of purchasers of insurance which are not authorized or are prohibited under state law.

file and use requirement: A state law which requires insurers to file property-casualty rates or forms with the regulator at the time their use commences, but does not require the regulator's prior approval. *See also* use and file *and* prior approval.

financial examination: A regulatory examination of the affairs of an insurer, focused on its financial condition. *See also* market conduct examination.

financial responsibility law: A state law which requires certain drivers or owners of automobiles to have prescribed minimum amounts of liability insurance.

Flesch Test: An arithmetic test for measuring the readability of a given text, such as an insurance policy.

flex rating: A system under state law which permits insurers to vary from filed and approved property-casualty rates, within certain percentage limits.

foreign insurer: From the point of view of a given United States jurisdiction, an insurer organized under the laws of another United States jurisdiction. *See also* domestic insurer *and* foreign insurer.

fronting: The issuance of policies by an admitted insurer in a given state and the simultaneous reinsurance of substantially all the risk under such policies with a non-admitted insurer.

FTC Act: See Federal Trade Commission Act.

GAAP: See generally accepted accounting principles.

generally accepted accounting principles: The principles of accounting which apply to most businesses, but not to the statutory financial condition of insurance companies. *See also* statutory accounting principles.

grace period: An additional period, such as 30 days, allowed in an insurance policy, and usually required by law, for the payment of premiums after their due date.

group insurance: Insurance provided to members of a group of persons, such as employees of a given employer, under a single group policy.

group policy or contract: An insurance policy or contract which provides coverage or benefits to members of a defined group of persons.

guaranty fund: A fund contributed to by solvent insurers, licensed in a given jurisdiction, to pay obligations of an insolvent insurer. *See also* post-assessment guaranty fund *and* pre-assessment guaranty fund.

health maintenance organization: A kind of health insurer which accepts prepayments from its members in exchange for providing medical services through its own staff and facilities.

HMO: See health maintenance organization.

IBNR: See incurred but not reported losses.

impaired insurer: An insurer whose financial condition is weak or impaired according to statutory criteria, but which is not insolvent.

incontestability: The inability of an insurer to contest the validity of a life or health insurance policy based on misrepresentation by the insured or policyholder.

incurred-but-not-reported losses (IBNR): Estimated amounts of claims payable by a property-casualty insurer based on accidents or other events which have happened but have not been reported to the insurer.

individual policy or contract: A policy or contract which directly covers an individual, as opposed to a group policy or contract which covers members of a group.

insolvent insurer: An insurer whose liabilities exceed its assets or which is unable to pay its obligations as they arise, in accordance with statutory criteria.

insurable interest: A lawful interest in the subject matter which makes an insurance contract legally enforceable.

Insurance Regulatory Information System (IRIS): A system of analyzing financial results, developed by the NAIC, which is intended to detect or predict impaired and insolvent insurers. Formerly called Early Warning System.

Insurance Services Offices, Inc. (ISO): An organization of property-casualty insurers which develops rating information and policy forms for its members in various states, for most lines of business other than workers' compensation and employers' liability.

involuntary market: A market consisting of coverages provided by insurers on a cooperative basis to insureds who cannot obtain them otherwise. *See also* voluntary market.

IRIS: See Insurance Regulatory Information System.

ISO: See Insurance Services Office, Inc.

joint underwriting association (JUA): A kind of assigned risk plan under which the member insurers' obligations are shared through an association or similar entity.

JUA: See joint underwriting association.

leeway provision: See basket provision.

lines of insurance: Different kinds of insurance, such as automobile liability or fire insurance, which an insurer must be separately licensed to sell.

liquidation: The distribution of an insolvent insurer's assets in payment of its liabilities under court supervision.

liquidator: An official appointed by a court to supervise the liquidation of an insurer.

Lloyds of London: See Underwriters at Lloyds.

loan value: See policy loan value.

loss costs: The projected cost of claim payments without expenses, based upon historical data. *See also* pure premiums.

MAP: See market assistance plan.

marine insurance: Insurance on vessels and other instrumentalities of navigation on water. *See also* casualty insurance and property insurance.

market assistance plan (MAP): An administrative agency of insurers which circulates applications for coverage to members in order to facilitate the writing of coverages for certain hard-to-place insureds.

market conduct examination: A regulatory examination of the business of an insurer, focused on how it does business with its policyholders. *See also* financial examination.

McCarran-Ferguson Act: A federal law, enacted in 1945, which authorizes the states to continue to regulate insurance and grants a limited antitrust immunity to the business of insurance.

Mini-McCarran Acts: State laws which exempt the insurance business to various degrees from the application of state antitrust laws.

minimum standards requirements: State laws or regulations which require certain minimum coverages and benefits in health insurance policies.

monoline insurer: An insurer licensed to sell only one line of insurance, such as title insurance. *See also* multiline insurer.

MSVR: See Mandatory Securities Valuation Reserve.

multiline insurer: An insurer licensed to sell more than one line of insurance, such as fire and marine insurance.

mutual insurer: An insurer which is owned by its policyholders, and which has no shareholders. *See also* stock insurer and reciprocal insurer.

mutualization: Conversion of an insurer from the stock form of ownership to the mutual form. *See also* demutualization.

NAIC: See National Association of Insurance Commissioners.

National Association of Insurance Commissioners (NAIC): An association of the insurance regulatory officials of the various states and territories of the United States which develops recommended laws and regulations, and establishes procedures for the regulation of the insurance business.

National Council on Compensation Insurance, Inc. (NCCI): An organization of property-casualty insurers which develops rating information and policy forms for its members in the field of workers' compensation and employers' liability insurance.

National Workers' Compensation Reinsurance Pool: A pool of member insurers which reinsures policies written under various state assigned risk plans for workers' compensation and employers' liability insurance.

NCCI: See National Council on Compensation Insurance, Inc.

Noerr-Pennington Doctrine: A rule of federal case law which gives antitrust immunity to cooperative business activities aimed at obtaining legislative or regulatory changes.

no-fault law: A state law which eliminates the right to sue for damages and instead provides insurance benefits for certain persons injured in automobile accidents.

non-admitted assets: Assets for which an insurer cannot legally take credit on its annual statement. *See also* admitted assets.

non-admitted insurer: An insurer not licensed to do business in a given jurisdiction. *See also* admitted insurer.

nonforfeiture law: A state law which requires insurers to provide cash and loan values under certain kinds of life insurance policies.

non-renewal: The refusal by an insurer to renew a property-casualty policy upon its expiration.

non-resident license: A license granted to an insurance agent or broker who is not a resident of the jurisdiction in question.

off-shore captive: A captive insurer organized under the laws of a non-U.S. jurisdiction, such as Bermuda. *See also* captive insurer *and* on-shore captive.

on-shore captive: A captive insurer organized under the laws of a United States jurisdiction. *See also* captive insurer *and* off-shore captive.

participating policy: A policy under which policy dividends may be payable to the insured, depending upon the insurer's financial results. *See also* policy dividend.

Paul v. Virginia: A case decided by the United States Supreme Court in 1869 in which it was held that insurance is not commerce subject to regulation by the federal government under the Constitution. *See also* South-Eastern Underwriters case.

policy cash surrender value: An amount of money payable to the policyholder upon termination of certain life insurance policies during the insured's lifetime.

policy dividend: A dividend payable by an insurer to its policyholders, as opposed to shareholders.

policy loan value: An amount of money which a policyholder is entitled to borrow against the cash surrender value of certain life insurance policies.

policyholder surplus: See surplus.

post-assessment guaranty fund: A guaranty fund under which assessments are made against members after the occurrence of an insolvency. *See also* guaranty fund.

pre-assessment guaranty fund: A guaranty fund under which assessments are made against members before the occurrence of an insolvency. *See also* guaranty fund.

preference: See preferential transfer.

preferential transfer: A payment or transfer by an insurer to a creditor, made within a certain statutory time period (usually four months) before its insolvency, which may be recovered by the receiver or liquidator for the benefit of all creditors.

premium financing: The business of lending money to pay insurance premiums, in which the lender obtains a lien or security interest in the policy or policies being financed.

premium taxes: Taxes imposed by state law on premiums received by insurers.

prior approval requirement: A type of rate or form filing requirement under which the regulator's approval is required before the insurer may use the rates or forms. *See also* file and use requirement *and* use and file requirement.

property insurance: Insurance against loss or destruction of property, such as buildings and their contents. *See also* casualty insurance *and* marine insurance.

purchasing group: A group of insureds in a common business or enterprise who purchase liability insurance on a group basis, as authorized by the federal Liability Risk Retention Act.

pure premiums: Amounts representing the cost of anticipated claims, not including profit or expense allowances. *See also* loss costs.

rating bureau: A synonym for rating organization. *See also* rating organization.

rating organization: A cooperative organization of member insurers which develops and files rates and forms for use by its members.

readability: A legal criterion relating to the purported relative ease of understanding an insurance policy. *See also* Flesch Test.

rebating: The illegal return of part of a premium or commission by an insurer or agent to an insured.

receiver: An official in control of the property and affairs of an insolvent insurer under court supervision. *See also* ancillary receiver *and* domiciliary receiver.

receivership: The control of the affairs of an insolvent insurer by a receiver under court supervision.

reciprocal insurer: An insurer consisting of member insureds and an attorney in fact who binds the members severally on policy risks. *See also* mutual insurer *and* stock insurer.

redlining: Unlawful discrimination in the underwriting of property or casualty risks based solely on their geographical location.

rehabilitation: The supervision of the affairs of an insurer by a court-appointed official in order to prevent or remedy insolvency without liquidating the insurer.

reinstatement: Putting a policy back in force by mutual agreement or under a reinstatement clause after a period of lapse.

reinsurance: Contractual transfer of risk from a direct insurer to a reinsurer.

reinsurance facility: A kind of residual market plan under which insurers may avail themselves of a guaranteed source of reinsurance.

reinsurance intermediary: A broker or similar intermediary who acts as such in the placing of reinsurance coverages between direct insurers and reinsurers.

replacement regulation: A state law or regulation under which certain comparative information and warnings must be given to policyholders who intend to replace existing life or health insurance coverage. *See also* twisting.

representations: See representations and warranties.

representations and warranties: Statements made by an applicant for insurance which may be the basis for denial of a claim if untrue.

reserves: Liabilities of an insurer based on the estimated cost of existing and future claims and other benefits.

residual market: Collectively, those risks which insurers are unwilling to insure voluntarily under the usual conditions. *See also* assigned risk plan.

retaliatory requirements: Foreign insurer licensing requirements of a given state which duplicate the comparable requirements of the foreign insurer's state of domicile.

retrocession: Transfer of risk from a reinsurer to another reinsurer, called a retrocessionaire.

risk retention group: An insurer created and owned by a group of businesses or public entities which are authorized by law to share liability risks among themselves.

SAP: See statutory accounting principles.

savings bank life insurance: Life insurance underwritten and sold by savings banks as authorized by law in some states.

SBLI: See savings bank life insurance.

schedule rating: The use of debits and credits in rating property-casualty risks, based on certain prospective risk characteristics, such as safety devices and programs.

seasoning requirement: A statutory or other regulatory requirement that an insurer have prior experience in a line of business in order to become licensed in another state.

Securities Valuation Manual: A periodical publication of the NAIC which lists the values of many different securities for annual statement purposes.

separate account: A financial account of the funds and investments held by a life insurer under variable or similar contracts.

Sherman Act: A federal antitrust law which generally prohibits contracts and combinations in restraint of trade.

South-Eastern Underwriters case: A case decided by the United States Supreme Court in 1944 in which it was held that insurance is commerce subject to federal regulation under the Constitution. *See also Paul v. Virginia.*

standard fire policy: A prescribed form of fire insurance policy required by New York and other states' laws.

state action doctrine: A rule of federal case law which exempts business activities required by law (such as uniform pricing) from the federal antitrust laws.

state insurance fund: A public entity established under state law to write property-casualty insurance coverages in competition with, or to the exclusion of, private insurers.

statement: See annual statement.

statistical plan: A mandatory plan under state law for the reporting of statistical information about premiums, losses, and expenses to a rating bureau or similar organization.

statutory accounting principles: The principles of accounting, established by state law, which govern the determination of a licensed insurer's financial condition for regulatory purposes. *See also* generally accepted accounting principles.

statutory deposits: Cash or securities of an insurer held in trust by a state regulator for the benefit of residents of the state.

stock dividend: A dividend payable by an insurer to its shareholders, as opposed to policyholders. *See also* policy dividend.

stock insurer: An insurer owned by shareholders, as opposed to policyholders. *See also* mutual insurer and reciprocal insurer.

surplus: An amount equal to an insurer's assets minus its liabilities and capital.

surplus lines: See excess and surplus lines.

treaty: A reinsurance agreement.

twisting: Replacement of life or health policies by an agent or broker using deceptive practices. *See also* replacement regulation.

Underwriters at Lloyds: An organization of underwriters, headquartered in London, who subscribe to risks in various shares.

unearned premium reserve: A liability of an insurer representing part of premiums received but not yet earned by the passage of time.

unfair trade practices act: A state insurance law which prohibits unfair competition and unfair and deceptive trade practices in the insurance business.

uninsured motorist fund: A fund established by state law to pay for damages incurred in automobile accidents caused by uninsured drivers.

unisex rating: The calculation and application of premium rates without regard to the sex of the insured.

use and file requirement: A requirement concerning rates or forms under which a filing must be made with the regulator within a certain time after use of the rate or form commences. *See also* file and use requirement *and* prior approval requirement.

variable contract: A life insurance policy or annuity contract under which values and benefits are based on the fluctuating value of an investment fund. *See also* separate account.

voluntary market: The usual market of insurers and insureds, as opposed to the assigned risk, residual, or involuntary market.

white list: A listing of excess and surplus lines insurers approved by the regulator in a given state. *See also* excess and surplus lines.

yellow book: A fire-casualty insurer's annual statement, the cover of which is usually yellow. *See also* blue book.

zone system: The system of insurer examinations adopted by the NAIC, under which some insurers are examined by teams of regulatory officials comprised of representatives from various states in certain geographical zones.

Further Reading

Abraham, Kenneth S. *Insurance Law and Regulation*. Westbury, N.Y.: Foundation Press, 1990.

Caddy, Douglas. *Legislative Trends in Insurance Regulation*. College Station: Texas A&M University Press, 1986.

Campbell, Dennis (Ed.). *International Insurance Law and Regulation*. London: FT Law and Tax, 1994.

Chance, Clifford. *Insurance Regulation in Europe*. London: Lloyds of London Press Ltd., 1993.

Ettlinger, Kathleen, Hamilton, Karen, and Krohm, Gregory. *State Insurance Regulation*. Malvern, Pa.: Insurance Institute of America, 1995.

Gart, Alan. *Regulation, Deregulation, Reregulation: The Future of the Banking, Insurance, and Securities Industries*. New York: John Wiley & Sons, 1994.

Hamilton, Karen. *The Changing Nature of Insurance Regulation*. Malvern, Pa.: Insurance Institute of America, 1995.

Hodgin, R. W. *Protection of the Insured*. London: Lloyds of London Press Ltd., 1989.

Kimball, Spencer. *Insurance and Public Policy*. Madison: The University of Wisconsin Press, 1966.

Kimball, Spencer, and Denenberg, Herbert S. (Eds.). *Insurance, Government, and Social Policy*. Homewood, Ill.: Richard D. Irwin, 1969.

Koike, Teije (Trans.). *Japanese Insurance Laws, Ordinances, and Regulations*. Tokyo: The Non-Life Insurance Institute of Japan, 1990.

Mantran, Julio Castelo (Rojas, deWahr, Hough, and Bourne, Trans.). *The Insurance Market in Latin America, Portugal, and Spain* (originally published as *El Mercado de Seguros en Latinoamerica, Portugal, y Espana*, Madrid: Editorial Mapfre S.A., 1972). Athens: University of Georgia Press, 1976.

McDowell, Banks. *The Crisis in Insurance Regulation*. Westport, Conn.: Quorum Books, 1994.

McDowell, Banks. *Deregulation and Competition in the Insurance Industry*. Westport, Conn.: Quorum Books, 1989.

Pellish, Harold. *Regulation of Insurance by the State of New York*. Ann Arbor, Mich.: University Microfilms, 1976.

Russ, Lee R., and Segalla, Thomas F. *Couch on Insurance 3d*. Deerfield, Ill.: Clark Boardman Callahan, 1995.

Semaya, Francine L., and Vitkowsky, Vincent J. (Eds.). *The State of Insurance Regulation*. Chicago: American Bar Association, Tort and Insurance Practice Section, 1991.

Index

Financial responsibility laws. *See* Automobile insurance
Foreign insurers, 87–88
Formation and organization of insurers, 19–23
Fronting, 103

Generally accepted accounting principles (GAAP), 33
Geographical discrimination, 106–107
Group life and health insurance, 60
Guaranty funds, 96–99

Health insurers, 21
Health maintenance organizations (HMOs), 23
Historical background of insurance regulation, 1–4
Holding companies, 81–83

Incorporation of insurers, 19–20
Independent adjusters, 78
Insolvency of insurers, 95–96
Insurable interest, 63
Insurance consultants, 78
Insurance contracts, 60–66; defined, 26–27
Insurance exchanges, 23–24
Insurance Regulatory Information Systems (IRIS), 50
Insurance Services Office (ISO), 54–55
Investments of insurers, 36–37

Joint underwriting associations (JUAs), 68–69

Liability Risk Retention Act, 11, 93
Licensing of agents and brokers, 74–75
Licensing of insurers, 25–31
Life and health insurers, 21
Life insurance cost disclosure, 108–109
Life insurance policies, 62
Life insurance replacement, 108–109
Life insurance reserves, 34–35
Liquidation of insurers, 96

Managing general agents, 77–78
Manuals of classifications, rules and rates, 55–56

McCarran-Ferguson Act, 3–6, 119–120
Medicare Supplement Insurance, 11
Mini-McCarran Acts, 6
Mutual insurers, 20–21

National Association of Insurance Commissioners (NAIC), 15–17
National Council on Compensation Insurance (NCCI), 54–56
Noerr-Pennington Doctrine, 6–7
No-fault automobile insurance, 65
Non-admitted insurers, 87–90
Nonforfeiture values, 62

Organization of insurers. *See* Formation and organization of insurers

Paul v. Virginia, 2–3
Premium financing, 109
Premium taxes, 112–113
Producers, 75
Property-casualty insurers, 21
Property-casualty reserves, 35–36
Public adjusters, 78
Purchasing groups, 93

Rates and rating organizations, 52–58
Readability, 61
Rebating of commissions, 78
Reciprocal insurers, 20
Redlining. *See* Geographical discrimination
Registered products, 10
Registration statements, 82
Reinsurance, 100–104
Reinsurance intermediaries, 77
Representative capacity of agents and brokers, 78–79
Reserves of insurers, 34–36
Residual market mechanisms. *See* Assigned risk plans
Retaliatory requirements, 30–31
Risk management alternatives, 90–93
Risk retention groups, 93

Savings Bank Life Insurance (SBLI), 24
Securities laws, 10
Self-insurance, 90–92

Separate accounts, 41
Social Security, 12
State Action Doctrine, 6
State taxation of insurers. *See* Taxation of
  insurers
Statistical reporting, 57–58
Statutory accounting principles, 33–34
Stock insurers, 20
Surplus, 38–39

Taxation of insurers, 111–113
Third-party administrators, 77–78
Trade practices, 105–106

Unfair claims and trade practices. *See*
  Trade practices

Uninsured motorist funds, 65–66
Unisex rating, 58
United States Constitution, 1–2, 117
*United States v. South-Eastern Under-
writers Association*, 2–3

Valuation of securities, 37–38
Variable insurance products, 10

Workers' compensation insurance, 54–56,
  69–70

Zone system of examinations, 47–49

About the Author

PETER M. LENCSIS is an attorney in private practice in New York City. Formerly Vice President and General Counsel of Greater New York Mutual Insurance Company, he has contributed to legal treatises in his field and has been a member of the adjunct faculty at The College of Insurance since 1987.

ISBN 1-56720-085-0

HARDCOVER BAR CODE